U.S. Fish & Wildlife Service

Florida Panther
National Wildlife Refuge

**Draft Comprehensive
Conservation Plan**

Florida Panther
National Wildlife Refuge
3860 Tollgate Blvd, Suite 300
Naples, FL 34114
Telephone: 941/353 8442
Fax: 941/353 8640

U.S. Fish & Wildlife Service
1 800/344 WILD
http://wwww.fws.gov

October 1998

Table of Contents

Draft Comprehensive Conservation Plan
Florida Panther National Wildlife Refuge

Appendices

Figures

Introduction

List of Preparers

U.S. Fish and Wildlife Service
Personnel
Jim Krakowski
Dennis Jordan
Ben Nottingham
Larry Richardson
Rick Kanaski
Andy Eller
Wendell Metzen
Roger Beckham
Jennifer Harris
Evelyn Nelson
James A. Clark

Alabama A&M University
Student Interns:
Fesaaha Grebremikal
Frederick Gardenier
Berrien Barks
Phillip West

Research Management
Consultants, Inc.
Louis J. Bridges

Purpose of and Need for the Comprehensive Conservation Plan
Under the provisions of the National Wildlife Refuge System Improvement Act of 1997, the Service is required to develop comprehensive conservation plans for all lands and waters of the National Wildlife Refuge System. These plans will guide management decisions and set forth strategies for achieving the purposes of each refuge unit. The National Environmental Policy Act ensures that the Service will assess the environmental impacts of any actions taken as a result of implementing the Comprehensive Conservation Plan.

This Draft Comprehensive Conservation Plan and appended Environmental Assessment has been prepared for the Florida Panther National Wildlife Refuge, Collier County, Florida. Its purpose is to identify the role that the refuge will play in support of the mission of the National Wildlife Refuge System; the South Florida Ecosystem; the recovery of the Florida panther; and the goals of the Florida Panther National Wildlife Refuge and how it will address public concerns for more access to the refuge.

The draft plan outlines issues, concerns, and opportunities expressed to the Service during a series of public meetings. It also provides a description of desired future conditions and proposes long-range guidance to accomplish the purpose of the refuge. This guidance is presented in a listing of refuge goals, objectives, and strategies resulting from an analysis of possible management alternatives. An environmental assessment of management alternatives may be found in Appendix A.

In its final form, the plan will serve as an operational guide for the refuge manager over the next ten to fifteen years.

The plan is also needed to:
- provide a clear statement of the desired future conditions when refuge purposes and goals are accomplished;
- provide refuge neighbors and visitors with a clear understanding of the reasons for management actions on and around the refuge;
- ensure that management of the refuge reflects policies and goals of the National Wildlife Refuge System;
- ensure that refuge management is consistent with federal, state, and county plans;
- provide long-term continuity in refuge management; and
- provide a basis for operation, maintenance, and capital improvement budget requests.

Panther tracks
USFWS photo by Larry W. Richardson

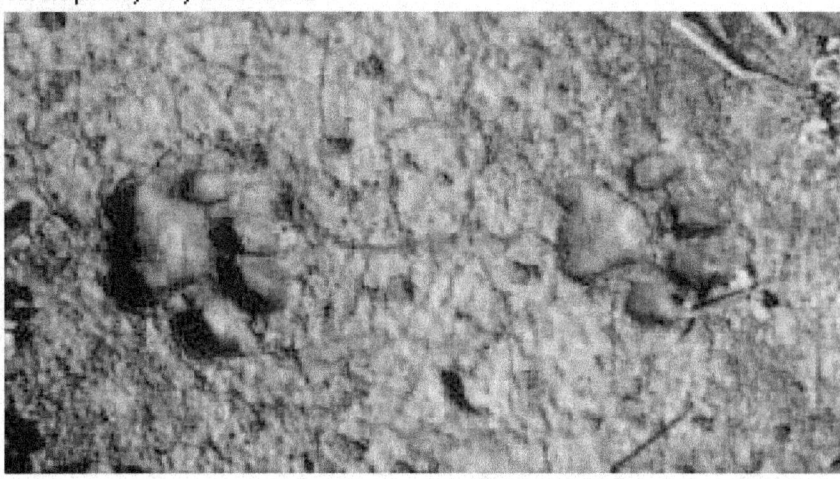

Overview of the Fish and Wildlife Service

The Fish and Wildlife Service is a federal bureau operated under the Department of the Interior, the Nation's principal conservation agency. The Department has responsibility for most of our nationally owned public lands and natural and cultural resources. This includes fostering wise use of our land and water resources, protecting our fish and wildlife, preserving the environmental and cultural values of our national parks and historical places, and providing for the enjoyment of life through outdoor recreation.

Figure 1. Organizational Chart of the Fish and Wildlife Service within the Department of the Interior

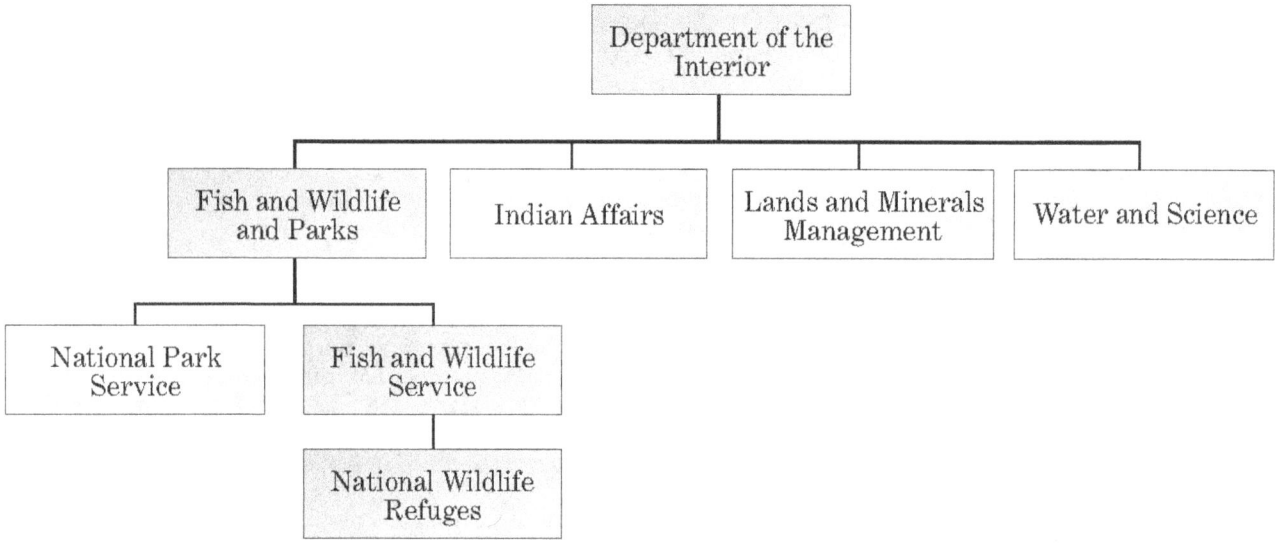

Mission of the Fish and Wildlife Service

The Fish and Wildlife Service is the principal organization through which the Department of the Interior carries out its responsibilities to conserve, protect, and enhance the nation's fish and wildlife and their habitats for the continuing benefit of people. The Service has major responsibility for migratory birds, endangered species, anadromous and inter-jurisdictional fish, and certain marine mammals.

Description and Mission of the National Wildlife Refuge System

The Service also manages the National Wildlife Refuge System, the world's largest collection of lands set aside specifically for the protection of fish and wildlife populations and habitats. More than 510 national wildlife refuges provide important habitat for native plants and many species of mammals, birds, fish, insects, amphibians, and reptiles. These refuges also play a vital role in preserving endangered and threatened species as well as offer a wide variety of recreational opportunities. Many have visitor centers, wildlife trails, and environmental education programs. Nationwide, more than 25 million visitors annually hunt, fish, observe and photograph wildlife, or participate in interpretive activities on national wildlife refuges.

The mission of the National Wildlife Refuge System is to administer a national network of lands and waters for the conservation, management, and where appropriate, restoration of the fish, wildlife, and plant resources and their habitats within the United States for the benefit of present and future generations of Americans.

The Florida Panther National Wildlife Refuge

Refuge Location

The refuge is located approximately 20 miles east of Naples, Florida. The south boundary of the refuge parallels Interstate 75 (Alligator Alley); the east boundary follows State Road 29. Private lands border the refuge on both the north and west. The refuge shares common boundaries with Big Cypress National Preserve (east) and Fakahatchee Strand State Preserve (south).

Figure 2. Refuge Vicinity Map

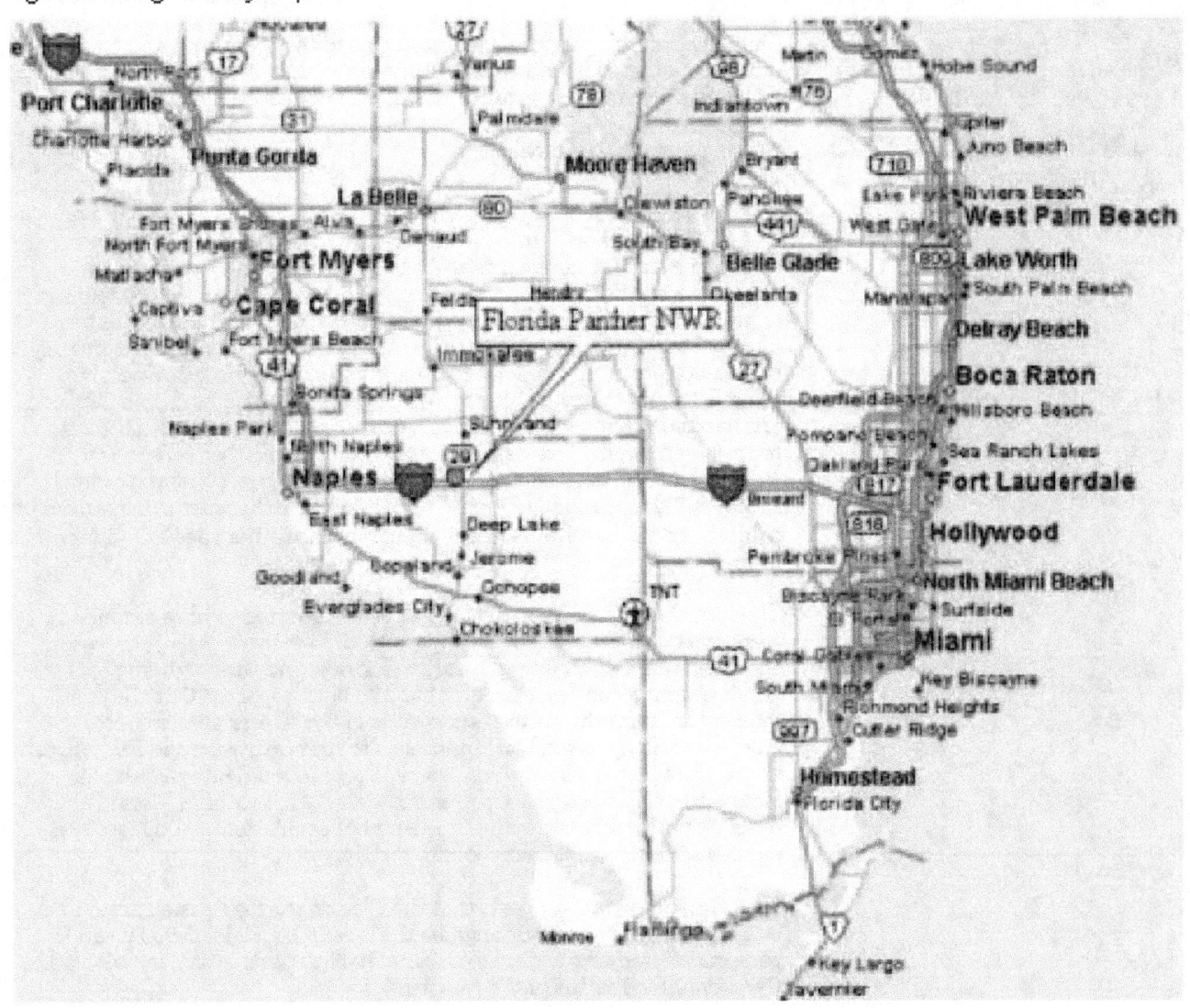

Florida panther
Photo by Don Pfitzer

Purpose of the Refuge

The refuge was established to conserve fish, wildlife, and plants which are listed as endangered and/or threatened species (Endangered Species Act of 1973). In addition, the refuge was established for the development, advancement, management, conservation, and protection of fish and wildlife resources (Fish and Wildlife Act of 1956).

The following two critical Service planning documents also played a strong role in defining the purpose of the refuge:

- First, the need and mechanism for establishing the refuge was provided in the 1986 "Fakahatchee Strand Environmental Assessment." This assessment clearly states that the refuge area should be acquired for the benefit and recovery of the endangered Florida panther.

- Second, the Service's 1995 "Florida Panther Recovery Plan," a document prepared by the interagency panther recovery team, states that the Florida Panther National Wildlife Refuge is essential to the survival of the panther and that the refuge should enhance habitat conditions for the panther and the panther's prey species.

Thus, the refuge's purpose has strong ties to the protection and recovery of the endangered Florida panther and its habitat. The refuge manager will give the panther greater consideration than other refuge species in management operations, and in making compatibility determinations relating to secondary uses.

The Florida Panther and Recovery Program

The Florida panther, Puma (Felis) concolor coryi, is one of the most endangered large mammals in the world. A single wild population in southern Florida, estimated to contain 30-50 adults, is all that remains of an animal that historically ranged throughout most of the southeastern United States. This population utilizes landscapes totaling approximately two million acres, approximately half of which is in private ownership. Panthers utilize all available native landscapes from upland pine flatwood and hardwood hammock forests to wetland systems dominated by wet prairies and swamp forests. For this reason, the panther serves as a "barometer" for the vast majority of other terrestrial plant and animal species endemic to south Florida. Preservation and proper management of habitats for the panther benefit vast numbers of other species indigenous to the ecosystem.

The historical distribution of the panther is reported to have extended west to Arkansas and Louisiana (possibly into eastern Texas); eastward across Mississippi, Alabama, Georgia, Florida, and the southern parts of South Carolina and Tennessee. It has also been reported that the panther intergraded with three other subspecies of the American puma; P.c. stanleyana to the west, P.c. hippolestes to the northwest, and P.c. cougar to the northeast. There are no historical population figures available. However, using the current population density in southern Florida as a basis for projection, the minimum historical population would have likely numbered from two to four thousand adults.

Historical literature suggests that the Florida panther was extirpated over much of its historical range by the late 1800s. Relentless human persecution (hunting and trapping), not habitat destruction, initially led to the endangered status of the panther.

By the time the panther was granted protection (State-1950 or Federal-1973), the taxon was already in danger of extinction throughout its historic range. Early recovery efforts focused around the Florida Game and Fresh Water Fish Commission's Florida Panther Clearinghouse and associated field surveys, initiated in the late 1970s. This effort focused on simply attempting to determine if a population of panthers still existed. These efforts led to the documentation of the population in southern Florida.

Intensive radio-instrumentation and monitoring was initiated in 1981. Since that time, 70 panthers have been instrumented and monitored producing a vast amount of biological and demographic information. (See Figure 3) Demographically, the population appears to function similar to mountain lion populations throughout occupied areas to the west. Physiologically, the population exhibits numerous manifestations attributed to generations of isolation and inbreeding. Environmental contaminants may also be contributing to some of these conditions.

Threats to the panther generally fall into three basic categories:
1. Population Security
The single, small population provides little security against extinction. In a population of this size, a disease outbreak or random fluctuations could reduce the population to a level to which it would be unable to sustain itself.

2. Population Viability
Population viability is threatened by numerous physiological and reproductive abnormalities prevalent within the population. For the most part, these conditions are considered manifestations of isolation and inbreeding, and possible environmental contamination. These include a high rate of abnormal sperm (90+ percent malformed), cryptorchidism (a testicle descending abnormality affecting 30-60 percent of males), congenital heart defects (including atrial septal defects), and possible immune deficiencies.

3. Habitat Destruction/Fragmentation/Contamination
Remaining panther habitat in south Florida is under tremendous threat from urban and agricultural conversion. Approximately half of the occupied landscape is under private ownership. It appears that habitats available to the radio-instrumented segment of the population in south Florida are at, or approaching, carrying capacity for the panther.

In 1986, the Florida Panther Interagency Committee was formed to provide for a cooperative, coordinated federal/state recovery program for the panther. The committee is made up of the Service, the National Park Service, the Florida Game and Fresh Water Fish Commission, and the Florida Department of Environmental Protection.

Recovery activities generally focus around the following three areas of emphasis:
1. Actions to protect, enhance, and monitor the existing population in south Florida, its associated habitats, and prey resources.
Agencies represented on the Florida Panther Interagency Committee focus on actions on their respective lands to enhance conditions for the panther. Approximately 900,000 acres of panther habitat on private lands have been identified in the Florida Panther Preservation Plan (Logan 1993). The plan classifies habitats as either Priority 1 or Priority 2, based on panther use and/or habitat quality (See Figure 4). Priority habitats are used most frequently by the panther and contain lands of high quality native habitat. Priority 2 habitats are used less frequently by the panther and represent lands of lower quality native habitat interspersed with intensive agriculture, serving as buffer zones to urban development and other forms of encroachment. Efforts are underway to design cooperative conservation programs that will compensate landowners for maintaining panther habitat on their lands.

2. Actions to address population health.
A genetic restoration program, designed to restore natural gene flow lost because of population isolation for a century or longer, was initiated in 1996. Eight P.c. stanleyana females were translocated into the population from southwest Texas. To date, eight intercross litters containing 12 verified kittens have been produced. Geneticists project that within a few generations, lost genetic variability and viability will be restored.

Florida panther kitten
USFWS photo by Larry W. Richardson

Florida panther at rest
Photo by R. H. Barrett

Figure 3. Florida Panther Distribution Map

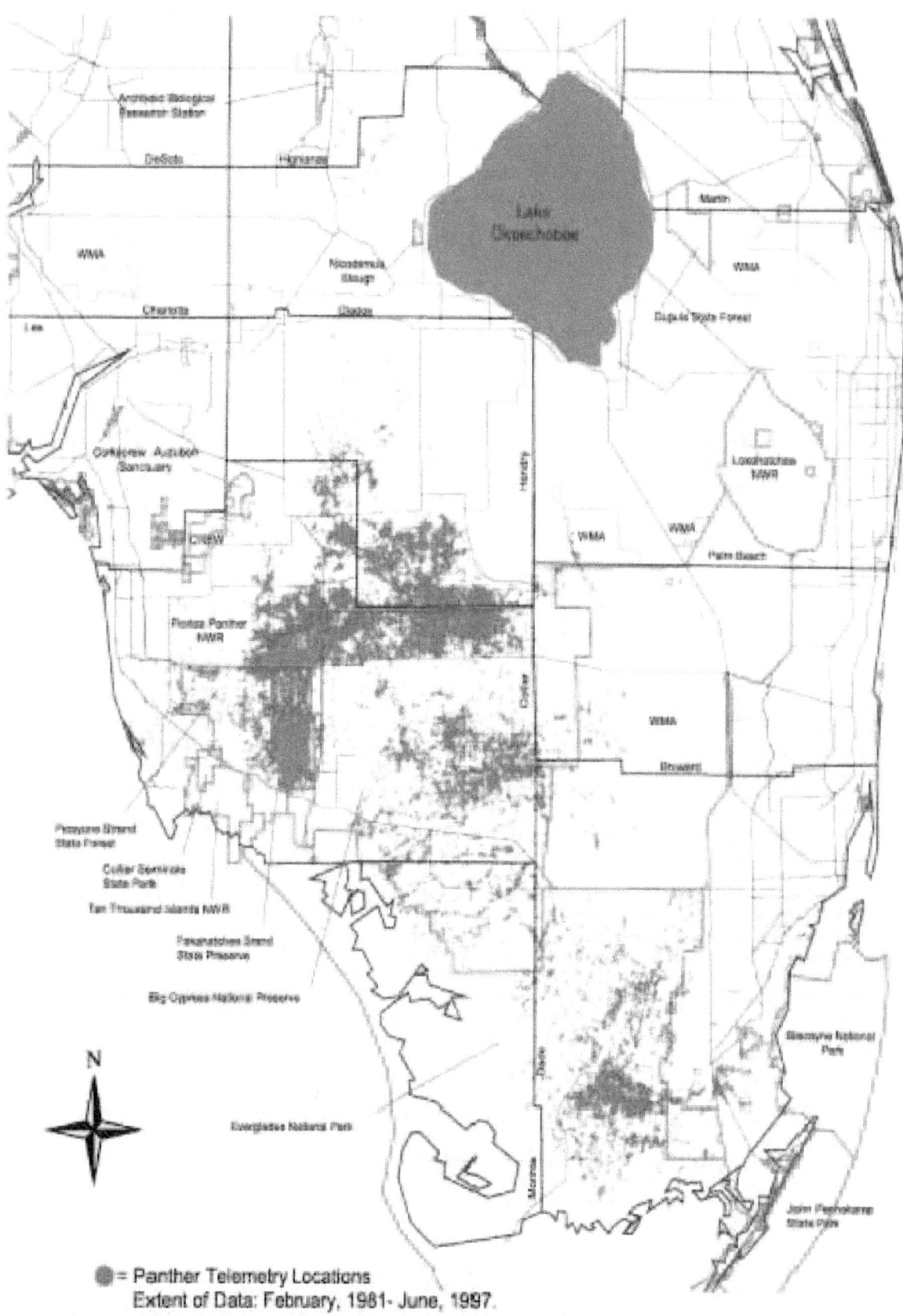

= Panther Telemetry Locations
Extent of Data: February, 1981- June, 1997.

Panther data compiled by the Florida Game and Fresh Water Fish Commission
and the National Park Service. Map produced by the U.S. Fish and Wildlife Service.

Figure 4. Priority Panther Habitats Map

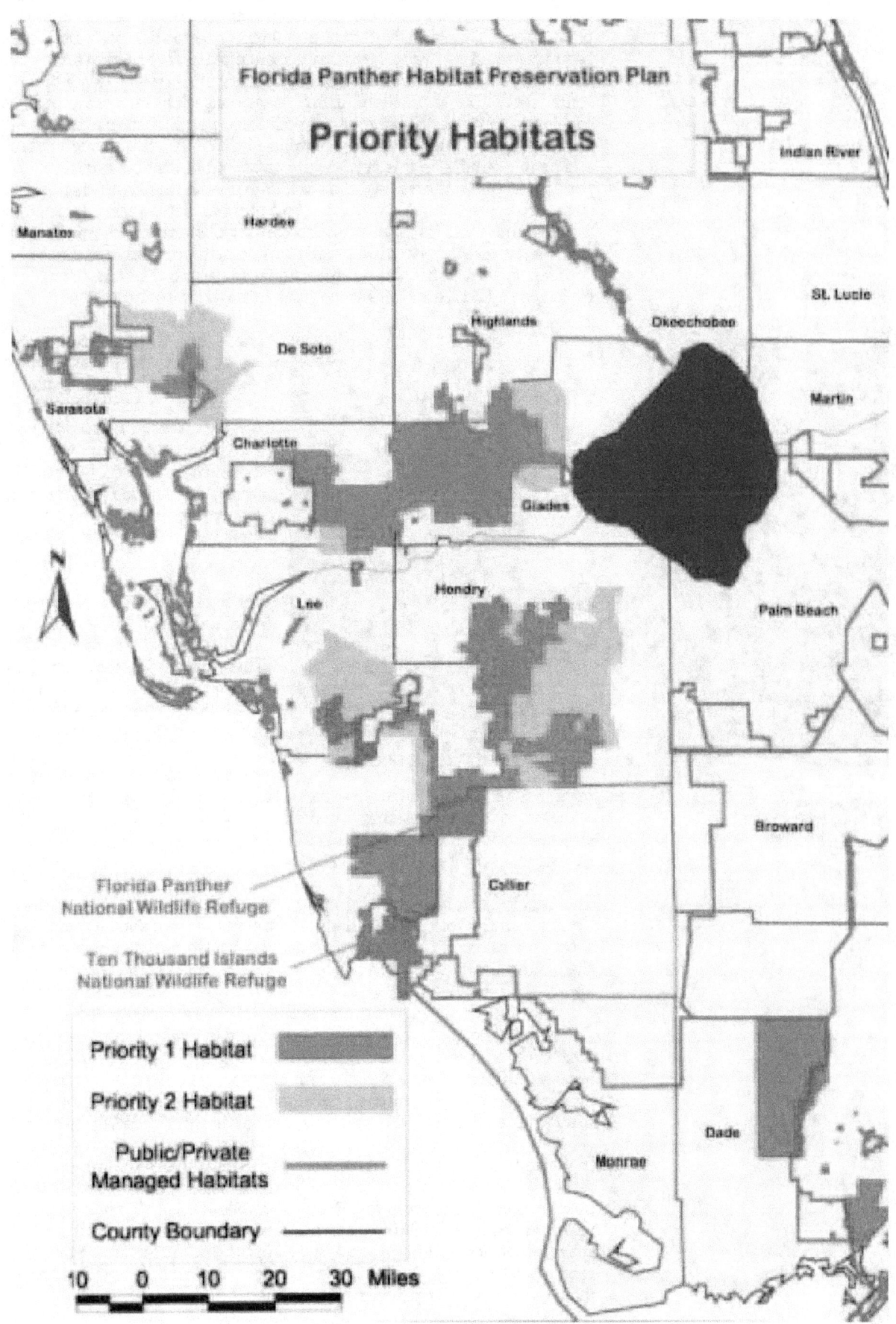

Florida Panther Habitat Preservation Plan

Priority Habitats

Legend:
- Priority 1 Habitat
- Priority 2 Habitat
- Public/Private Managed Habitats
- County Boundary

10 0 10 20 30 Miles

3. Actions to reestablish the panther into historic range areas.
The current recovery objective is to achieve a minimum of three viable, self-sustaining populations within the historic range of the panther. To reach this goal, at least two populations will have to be reestablished populations. Fourteen candidate population reestablishment sites have been identified in a preliminary site identification/evaluation effort. A recently completed reintroduction feasibility study within a north Florida/south Georgia candidate site, using Texas cougars as surrogate panthers, concluded that reestablishment of additional panther populations is biologically feasible. The study concluded that there are enough habitat and prey available in this site to support a viable, self-sustaining population of panthers. Based on preliminary evaluations, other candidate sites also appear capable of supporting panther populations. It now appears that the most significant remaining obstacle to advancing panther recovery is effectively dealing with sociological/political issues related to population reestablishment, which surfaced during the study. A program to evaluate and address these issues was initiated in early 1998.

Florida sunset
Photo by D. W. Pfitzer

The future of the panther looks brighter now than at any time since recovery efforts began in the late 1970s. The genetic restoration program proved successful and the reintroduction feasibility study has shown that habitats exist within the panther's historic range capable of supporting reestablished populations.

History of the Refuge
The Florida Panther National Wildlife Refuge was established in June 1989 by the authority of the Endangered Species Act to protect the important Florida panther. The final recovery plan for the panther was approved by the Service in December 1981. The plan stated ". . . it is vital to acquire the remainder of the Fakahatchee Strand and the prairies and cypress forests adjacent to it to ensure that a unified management strategy can be effected between the Fakahatchee Strand, the Big Cypress National Preserve, and the Everglades National Park."

The Service purchased the initial 24,300 acres of the refuge from the Collier Family (for which Collier County was named) for $10.3 million through a series of fee title acquisitions. With the addition of lands from the Collier Land Exchange on December 18, 1996, the refuge grew to approximately 26,400 acres.

The refuge encompasses the northern origin of the Fakahatchee Strand which is the largest cypress strand in the Big Cypress Swamp drainage basin. Orchids and other rare swamp plants grow within the strand's interior. The refuge contains a diverse mix of pine forests, cypress domes, marl prairies, hardwood hammocks, and lakes surrounded by swamps.

In addition to the panther, 20 other species of animals are found in the refuge vicinity that are state or federally listed as endangered, threatened, or species of special concern. The Florida black bear, alligator, wood stork, roseate spoonbill, limpkin, eastern indigo snake, Florida grasshopper sparrow, Everglades mink, and Big Cypress fox squirrel are a few examples. Other resident wildlife include whitetail deer and feral hogs, which are important panther prey species.

Common moorhen
USFWS photo by Larry W. Richardson

Role of the Refuge

The Florida Panther National Wildlife Refuge was established under the authority of the Endangered Species Act to protect Florida panther habitat. The refuge receives heavy use by this critically endangered species. During any given month, 5-11 panthers utilize refuge habitat areas. The refuge contains significant portions of the home ranges of several panthers and also functions as a vital habitat linkage for panthers utilizing adjacent portions of the Big Cypress National Preserve and Fakahatchee Strand State Preserve. Several female panthers have denned and raised kittens on the refuge in recent years. The refuge plays an important role in the restoration of the South Florida Ecosystem.

Refuge Function within the Ecosystem, and Ecosystem Priorities

The South Florida Ecosystem encompasses more than 16.5 million acres of richly diverse habitats covering the 19 southernmost counties in Florida. It is a subtropical region that lies between the Caribbean and temperate North America. (See Figure 5) Environmental and economic impacts of urbanization and agriculture, as well as other human activities, have altered the critical natural balance between land and water, and the region's endemic flora and fauna. Today, the South Florida Ecosystem faces substantial loss of habitat and fragmentation.

The Departments of Interior, Commerce, Army, Justice and Agriculture, and the Environmental Protection Agency created the South Florida Ecosystem Restoration Task Force for the purpose of halting or reversing ecological degradation. The task force has now expanded to include the State, Native American tribes, and the Governor's Commission for a Sustainable South Florida. The refuge plays an important role in integrating the requirements of the Interagency Agreement on South Florida Ecosystem Restoration and the mission of the National Wildlife Refuge System.

The following priorities have been determined by the Service for the South Florida Ecosystem, which includes the refuge:
- Protect and manage units of the National Wildlife Refuge System and other national interest lands.
- Protect migratory birds and protect, restore, and manage their habitats.
- Protect, restore, and manage candidate, threatened, and endangered species and their habitats.
- Protect, restore, and manage wetlands and other freshwater habitats.
- Protect, restore, and manage fish and other aquatic species and their habitats.
- Protect, restore, and enhance coastal and estuarine habitats.
- Protect, restore, and manage for biodiversity.

Great egrets, Roseate spoonbills, and Glossy ibis
Photo by Don Pfitzer

Figure 5. South Florida Ecosystem Map

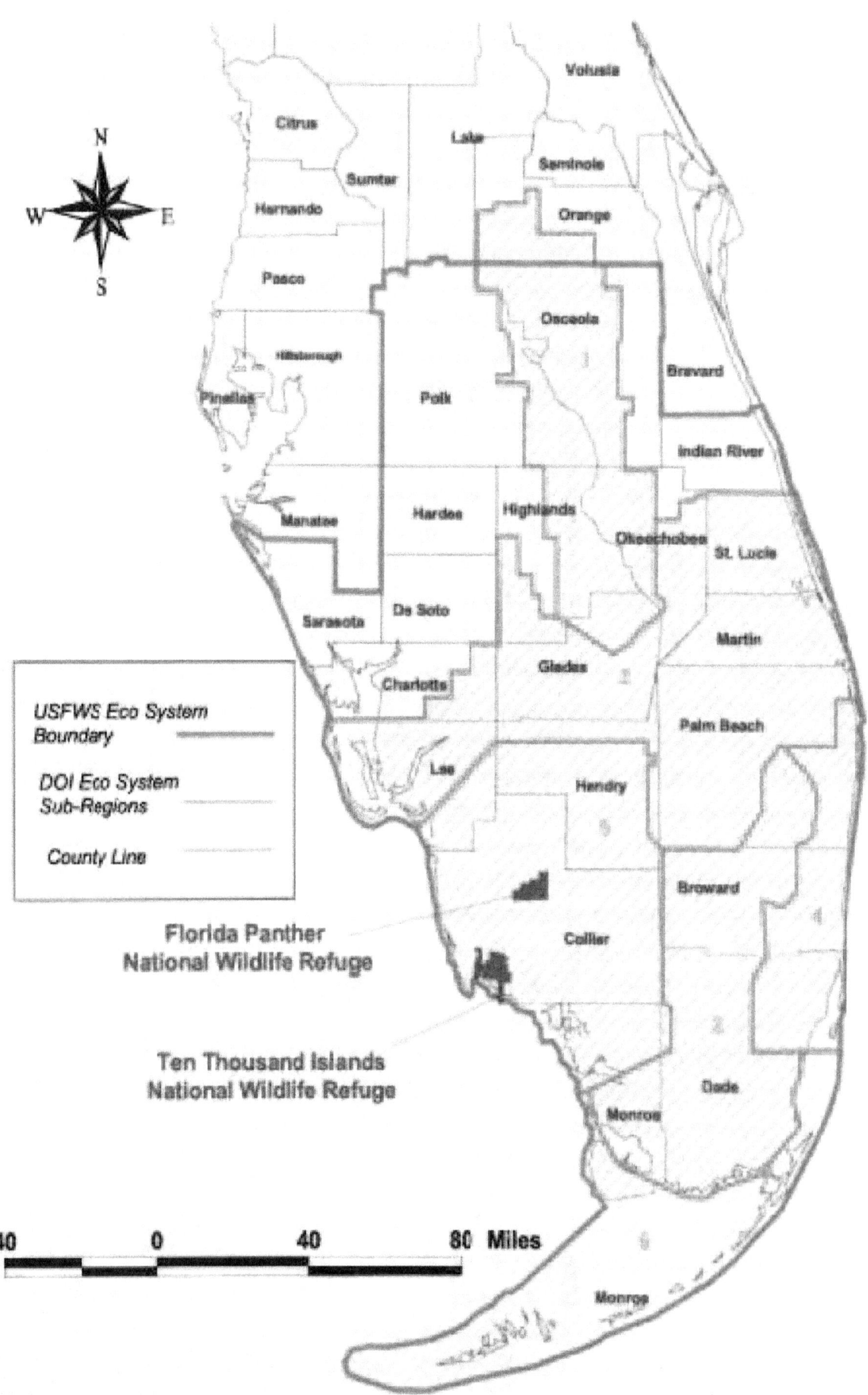

USFWS Eco System Boundary

DOI Eco System Sub-Regions

County Line

Florida Panther
National Wildlife Refuge

Ten Thousand Islands
National Wildlife Refuge

40   0   40   80 Miles

Legal Policy, Administrative Guidelines, and Other Considerations
Administration of national wildlife refuges is governed by various
International treaties, federal laws, Presidential Executive Orders and
regulations affecting land and water as well as the conservation and
management of fish and wildlife resources. Policies for management
options of the refuge are further refined by administrative guidelines
established by the Secretary of the Interior and policy guidelines
established by the Director of the Fish and Wildlife Service.

Select legal summaries of treaties and laws relevant to administration of
the National Wildlife Refuge System and management of the refuge are
provided in Appendix B.

Refuge Agreements
The refuge also operates under the following agreements with other
federal, state, and local entities:

Cooperative Agreement between the South Florida Water Management
District and Department of the Interior, Fish and Wildlife Service, and
Golden Florida Resort, Inc., a Florida Corporation, d/b/a Port of the
Islands Resort and Marina (for operation of multi-agency visitor center);

Cooperative Agreement between
the South Florida Water
Management District and
Department of the Interior, Fish
and Wildlife Service for the
construction of a water control
structure on Merritt Canal. Project
designed to restore hydrology to
Lucky Lake and Stumpy strands.

Interagency Agreement between
the Department of the Interior, Big
Cypress National Preserve and
Florida Panther National Wildlife
Refuge (for law enforcement);

Local Operational Agreement
between the Big Cypress National
Preserve and Florida Panther
National Wildlife Refuge and Ten
Thousand Islands National Wildlife
Refuge (for wildfire suppression and
prescribed burning);

Woodstorks
USFWS photo by Larry W. Richardson

Memorandum of Understanding between the Department of the Interior
and the State of Florida, Department of Environmental Protection (for
wildfire suppression and prescribed burning);

Memorandum of Understanding between the Department of the Interior
and the State of Florida, Department of Agricultural and Consumer
Services, Florida Division of Forestry (for wildfire suppression and
prescribed burning).

Planning Issues And Opportunities

Overview of the Public Involvement Process

Issue identification provides a sound basis for initiating the development of management objectives and strategies. To ensure that the future management of the refuge is reflective of the issues, concerns, and opportunities expressed by the public, a variety of scoping mechanisms was used.

- A survey was used to gather general information on current and potential refuge operations.
- Personal interviews were conducted during public scoping meetings.
- Letters were mailed to affected and interested publics to inform them of the planning process and invite their participation.
- A series of stakeholder meetings and community forums were held to develop components of the draft plan. The meetings and forums also allowed for consensus testing on the components of the plan developed by the stakeholder group and Service team. All stakeholder meetings and community forums were advertised and opened to the public.

A summary of the scoping and public involvement process is provided in Appendix C.

Scope of Issues, Concerns, and Opportunities

The following key issues, concerns, and opportunities were identified during the scoping process:

- **Public Access** - A major issue voiced by the public regarding access to the refuge. Traditionally, the refuge has been closed to public access with the exception of limited, small group tours. The public would like to have access to the refuge.
- **Cooperative Land Management and Partnerships** - The refuge is one of many public land management areas that along with private land interests make up the Big Cypress Watershed. Management actions in one part of the watershed may adversely impact other parts of the system. There was an overwhelming stakeholder desire to have the watershed cooperatively managed.
- **Public Awareness** - Survey respondents indicated an interest in knowing more about the panther and refuge programs.
- **Panther Habitat Protection on Private Lands** - A sizeable portion of important habitat used by the panther exists on private lands. Although land owners are not interested in selling their land, they are interested in maintaining natural areas.
- **Refuge Research and Management** - Research and habitat management are considered important tools to successfully manage the refuge.
- **Lack of Adequate Staffing** - There are not enough staff members to undertake initiatives needed to address Service responsibilities for the refuge and/or the South Florida Ecosystem.
- **Oil and Gas Exploration** - Oil and gas exploration exists on the refuge and produces an adverse affect on the resources.

All public issues, concerns, and opportunities for refuge management have been addressed in Appendix C, and in the development of comprehensive goals, objectives, and strategies. For the purposes of the draft management plan, special emphasis is placed on refuge access.

Great egrets
USFWS Photo by B. Gill

Proposed Management Direction

Refuge Mission
The mission of the Florida Panther National Wildlife Refuge is to conserve and manage lands and waters in concert with other agency land efforts within the Big Cypress Watershed, primarily for the Florida panther, other endangered and threatened species, natural diversity, and cultural resources for the benefit of the American people.

Refuge Vision Statement
The Florida Panther National Wildlife Refuge, as a vital link in the recovery of the panther, will be managed for the conservation of the panther, its habitat, other threatened and endangered species, natural diversity, and compatible uses. The refuge will be a model of effective collaboration in natural resource management and education among diverse public interests, public and private landowners on a voluntary basis, and agencies.

The Proposed Management Action
The proposed management action for the refuge is discussed in the following pages. The alternatives considered and their impacts, along with the impacts of the proposed action, are described in Appendix A.

Utilizing an Ecosystem Approach to manage the refuge is most preferred as it ideally meets the needs of the resources, and allows some access to the public for wildlife observation and environmental education. In addition, the Service plans to study the compatibility and feasibility of allowing hunting and fishing to occur on the refuge. The basis of this proposed action was developed from stakeholder consensus and as a result of public forums held during the planning process.

The end result is a set of goals, objectives, and strategies related to key issues that will guide the management of the refuge.

Ecosystem Approach
Public Access:
The refuge was established to provide habitat for the endangered Florida panther. The panther is the most endangered large animal in existence in the United States. Secondary access and the level of use for activities such as hunting, fishing, wildlife observation, wildlife photography, and recreational and interpretive trails on the refuge would depend greatly on their potential impacts to the panther and other resources. A decision to allow or disallow secondary use activities would depend upon whether or not these uses would have an adverse affect on the panther or other natural resources of the refuge.

Utilizing an ecosystems approach, the day-to-day management of the refuge would not change significantly. Opportunities for increased public use and recreational activities would be evaluated for implementation. However, three specific projects would be implemented to provide increased access near or within the refuge.

■ A short interpretive trail, 1/2 to 3/4 mile in length and placed in an area of least use by panthers, would not adversely affect the animal and would greatly promote awareness of refuge programs and the plight of the panther. The trail would contain interpretive and educational exhibits and would be for day-use only. Parking and waterless restroom facilities would be provided at the trail head. This form of access would be allowed and developed immediately.

Figure 6. Proposed Interpretive Foot Trail

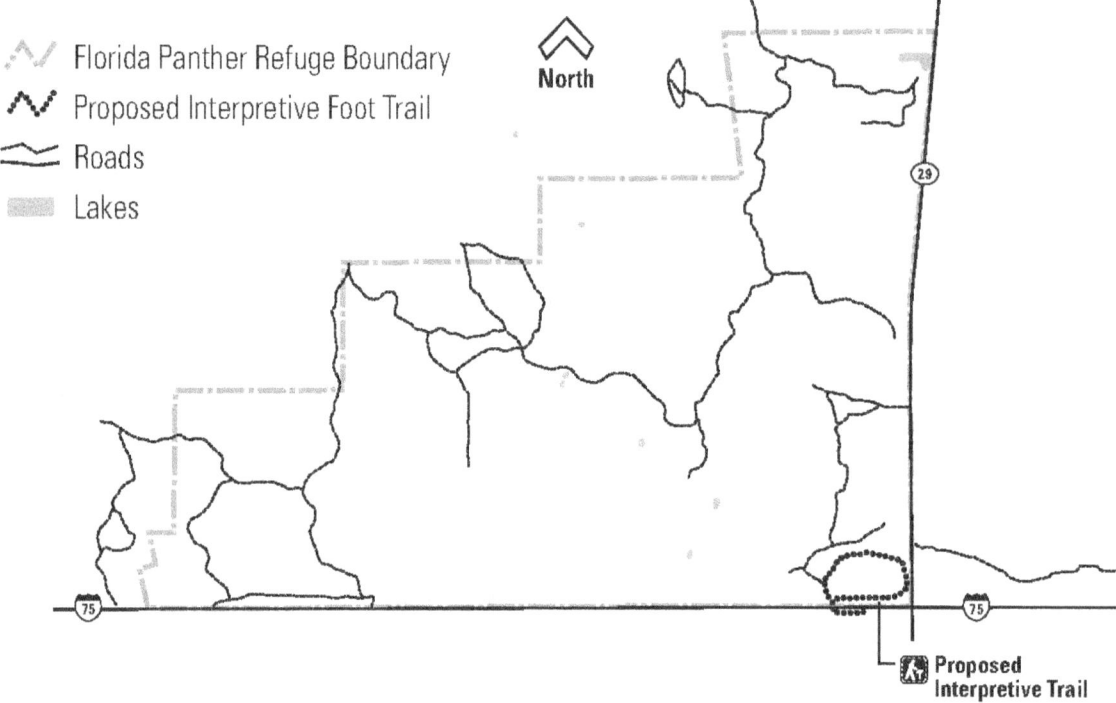

■ A second public access area would be developed in association with the waterbird habitat project, which is located on the east side of the refuge near SR 29. This project also would not adversely affect the panther and would help educate the public of the many birds that use the refuge. This project would include the development of a parking area, waterless restroom facilities, interpretive exhibits, and observation decks. The wildlife viewing area would also be for day-use only.

Figure 7. Proposed Waterbird/Wildlife Viewing Area

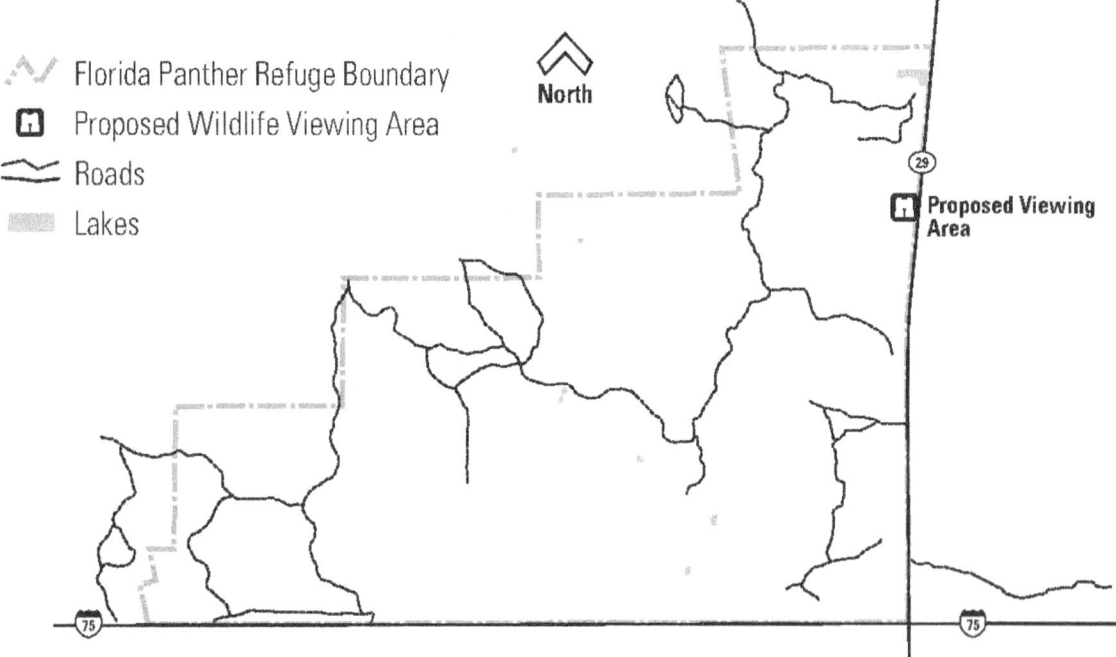

■ The Service, in partnership with other agencies, is seeking to offer a multi-agency visitor and environmental education center adjacent to the SR 29 and I-75 interchange. Strategies have been developed in the plan to pursue the installation of a facility of this nature.

Figure 8. Proposed Milti-Agency Visitor Center

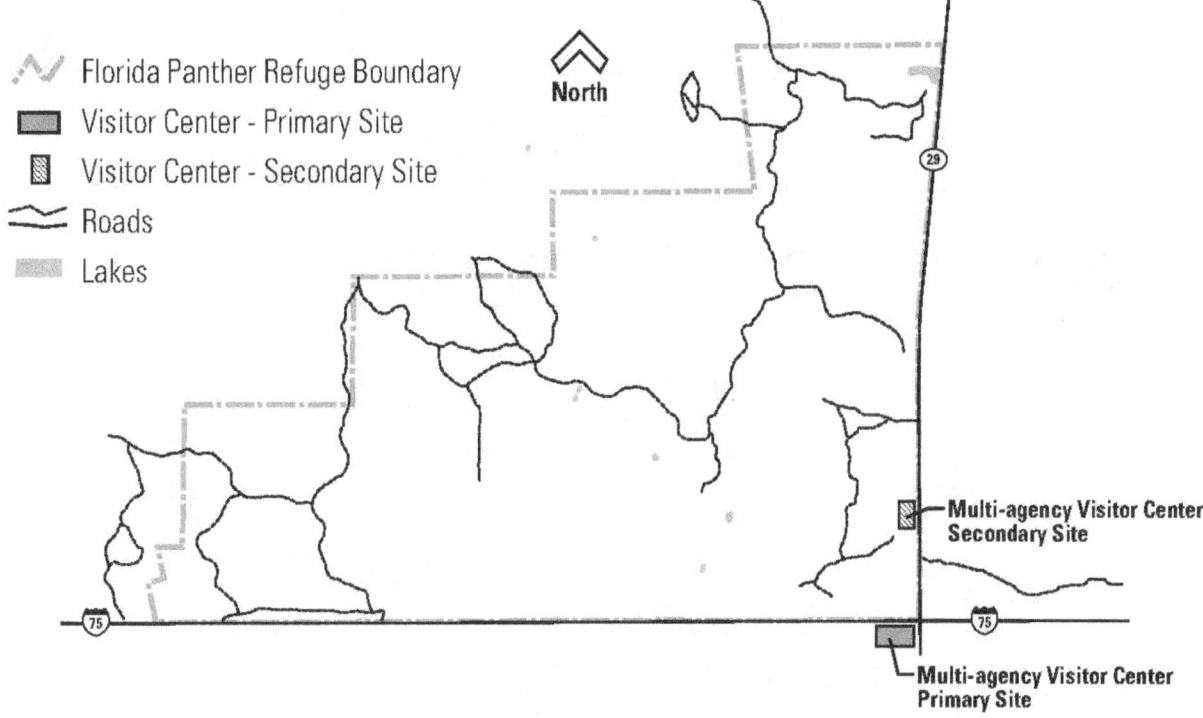

The Service will review suggested public access programs/activities within five years. Some decisions may take place before or after the 5-year period depending upon the results of studies and monitoring. Most of this research will be contracted out to universities. The Service cannot predict whether or not studies will be funded; if they occur in a timely manner; or, if the research will produce the results needed to make decisions.

Cooperative Land Management and Partnerships within the Big Cypress Watershed:
Considerably more emphasis would be placed on working with the local community, private landowners, non-governmental organizations, and other agencies in southwest Florida. Primary emphasis would be placed on developing partnerships with various entities that would lead to panther habitat protection and overall land and watershed protection and stewardship of the resources. More communication and coordination with other land managers within the watershed must occur if we are to effectively conserve the diverse resources of this ecosystem.

Habitat management on and off the refuge would be centered around watershed resources for the protection and enhancement of native wildlife populations, the panther, and other threatened, endangered, or candidate species that rely on wetlands. These areas benefit humans by being flood retention areas, water filters and drinking water recharge zones. A geographic information specialist and a hydrologist would be recruited to gather and evaluate watershed information.

More outreach efforts off the refuge would occur under this proposed action. A public use/environmental education specialist would work with the Collier County Environmental Education Consortium, school groups, volunteers, and other agencies to educate both youth and adults of southwest Florida about the panther and refuge activities. Furthermore, a media specialist would ensure the same message was delivered to the public by way of the media.

Protect Panther Habitat on Private Lands:
Habitat important to the panther is also critical to many other plants and animals. Added protection of panther habitat would be facilitated through conservation easements, tax breaks, mitigation banks, or some type of monetary incentive for the landowner to keep critical panther habitat in its natural state. The refuge would work in collaboration with public and private landowners, on a voluntary basis, to help insure the protection of 370,000 acres of panther habitat north of the refuge in Collier and Hendry counties.

Figure 9. Important Lands Eligible for Voluntary Panther Protection* as identified in the 1993 Florida Panther Preservation Plan. Priority 1 and Priority 2 habitats have been identified on page 6.

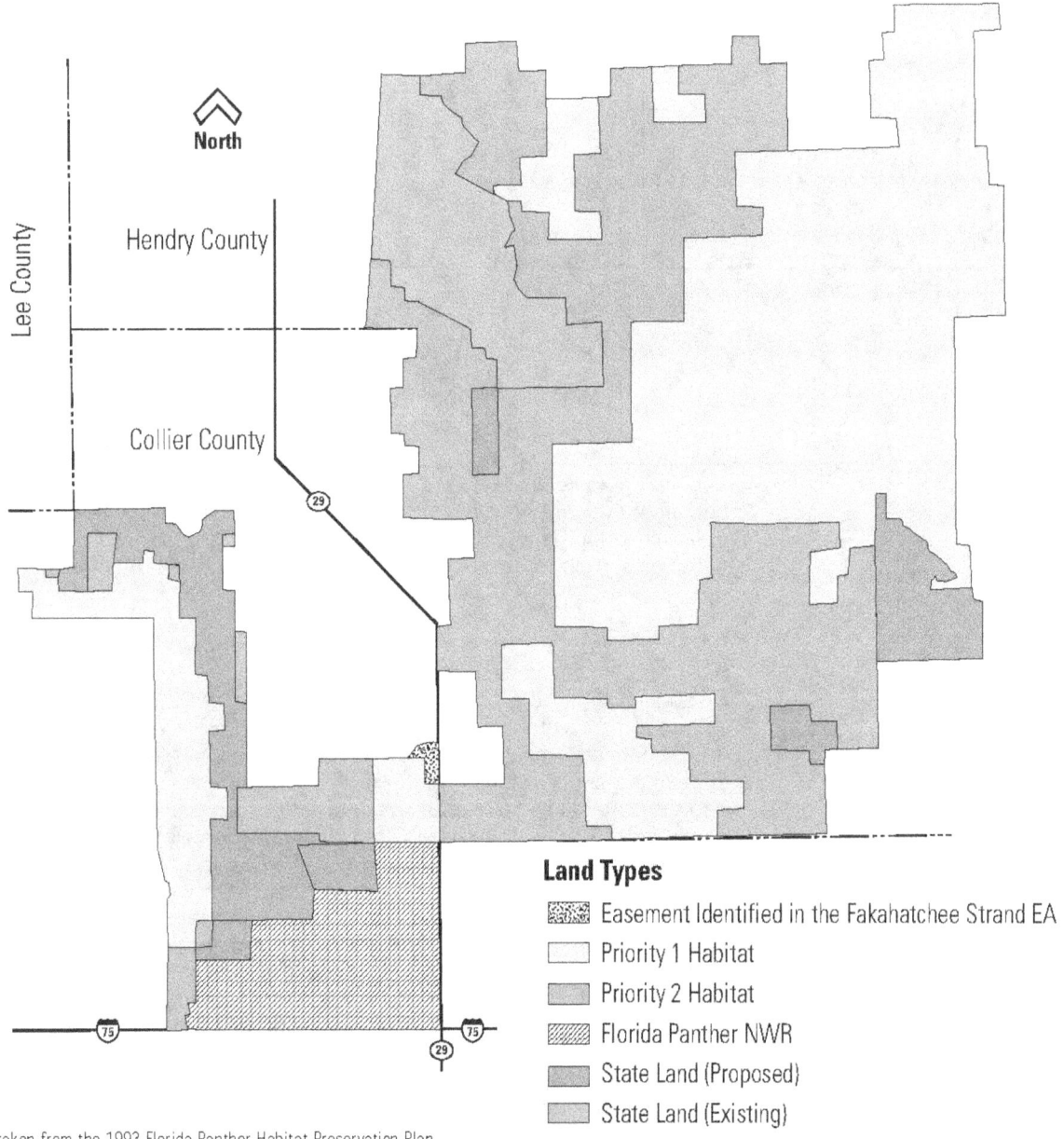

Land Types

▨ Easement Identified in the Fakahatchee Strand EA

☐ Priority 1 Habitat

▨ Priority 2 Habitat

▨ Florida Panther NWR

▨ State Land (Proposed)

▨ State Land (Existing)

*Map taken from the 1993 Florida Panther Habitat Preservation Plan

This would be a voluntary program for landowners. Through a variety of federal cost-share and wetland protection programs, the refuge would promote and coordinate ecosystem restoration projects within the watershed to include limited hydrologic restoration, the restoration of selected plant communities, and the limited reintroduction of endangered species.

This collaborative effort will involve a cooperative effort between state, federal, non-governmental organizations and private landowners to protect panther habitats existing on private lands. The goal is to initiate a conservation easement/lease program to protect essential panther habitat identified in the 1993 Panther Habitat Protection Plan. This project has two components. One part of the program would protect, through conservation easement, approximately 10,000 acres of priority panther habitat previously identified in the Fakahatchee Strand Environmental Assessment of 1985. These lands lie adjacent to the present refuge boundary to the north and west. The other part of the program would target at least 360,000 acres to be protected under term easement, or perpetual conservation easements. The project would involve only those landowners who are willing participants. Some of these areas may be considered for fee title ownership if they become available through donation, mitigation bank, or sale. This project would work in concert with other programs to protect habitats and wetlands within the Big Cypress Watershed. The easements would be monitored by a biologist working on the refuge staff. The estimated cost of the easements is $150 million. The biologist's salary, benefits, and equipment needs would require $100,000/year.

Refuge Research and Management:
Prescribed burning and exotic plant control would also be continued for ecosystem maintenance. Off-refuge efforts for prescribed burning, wildlife suppression, and invasive exotic species control would be enhanced. Refuge research and management would target topics that could be applied to management or have utility to other land managers within the ecosystem.

Lack of Adequate Refuge Staff:
With adequate staffing the refuge would meet Service and South Florida Ecosystem responsibilities. Education and outreach programs would be expanded. There would be increased coordination with land managers off the refuge through the initiation of conservation easements for important panther habitats. The biological and habitat monitoring program would be enhanced to include floral and faunal species that have not been monitored.

Gas and Oil Exploration:
The refuge would carefully review and minimize gas and oil exploration plans and operations, moreover, it would make every effort to gain mineral rights to oil and gas resources found on the refuge.

Refuge Management Goals
1.0   Provide optimum habitat conditions for the Florida panther with special consideration for other endangered and threatened species.
2.0   Restore and conserve the natural diversity, abundance, and ecological function of refuge flora and fauna.
3.0   Develop and implement an educational program that will provide an understanding and appreciation of the Florida panther, fish and wildlife ecology, and human influence on ecosystems of south Florida.
4.0   Promote interagency and private landowner cooperation for the management of natural and cultural resources within the Big Cypress Watershed.
5.0   Protect refuge cultural resources in accordance with federal and state historic preservation legislation and regulations.
6.0   Provide opportunities for compatible public use in accordance with the National Wildlife Refuge System Improvement Act of 1997.

Goals, Objectives, and Strategies to Support the Proposed Management Action

The following list of goals, objectives, and strategies will be used to implement the proposed management action. They were developed to reflect the needs of both the Service and the public (issues and opportunities). The listing of goals, objectives, and strategies specifies what the refuge manager will do, if funding requirements are met, as well as the exact activities to produce the desired results. Thus, the breakdown of activities forms a hierarchy for refuge management that also encompasses the mission of the Service, the refuge system, ecosystem priorities, the refuge's purpose, and the expressed needs of the public.

Figure 10. Hierarchy of Goals, Objectives, and Strategies

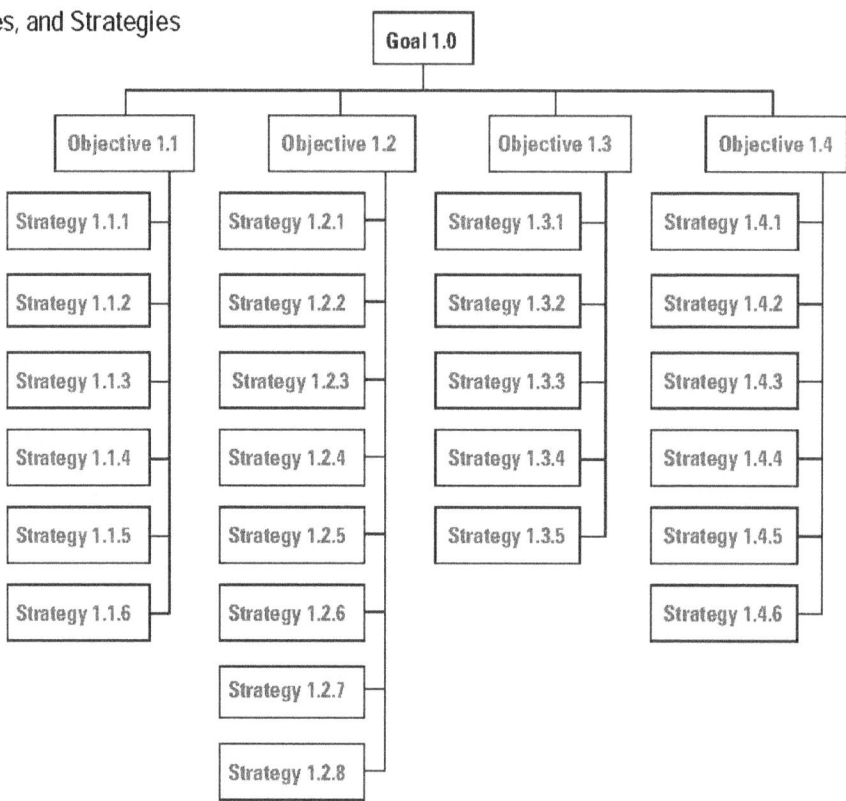

1.0   Provide optimum habitat conditions for the Florida panther with special consideration for other endangered and threatened species.

    1.1   Achieve and maintain vegetative conditions on the refuge and in southwest Florida that is preferred by the panther.

        1.1.1   Increase staff in order to rehabilitate equipment and maintain support facilities. Upgrade equipment as needed in order to support field operations. (Special Projects 1 and 2)

        1.1.2   Using Geographic Information System (GIS) technology and historic use data, characterize vegetative characteristics of preferred panther habitat (by use-type where possible, i.e., denning, day bedding, hunting, travel corridors, important habitat linkages, etc.).

        1.1.3   Determine panther response to prescribed fire management through ongoing funded research with U.S. Geological Survey, Biological Resource Division, University of Tennessee. Obtain results and evaluate findings by the end of 1998.

1.1.4 Refine refuge prescribed fire program and other habitat management tools to achieve and maintain optimum vegetative conditions for panther habitation.

1.1.5 By 2005, strive to achieve perpetual protection of approximately 10,000 acres of panther habitat adjacent to the refuge through fee title or easement acquisition.

1.1.6 By 2010, strive to achieve limited and perpetual protection of approximately 370,000 acres through conservation easement or fee title acquisition.

1.2. Achieve and maintain optimum prey densities for the Florida panther by the year 2007.

1.2.1 Conduct inventories to establish current deer density estimates for the refuge.

1.2.2 Follow approved Fire Management Plan to maintain/ enhance deer habitat. Conduct prescribed burns in a mosaic pattern within fire-evolved habitats to achieve a minimum target goal of 6,000 acres annually.

1.2.3 By 1999, evaluate the feasibility and potential value of establishing small ponds in areas where water is seasonally absent or scarce. If feasible, a minimum of 10 ponds will be established by 2002.

1.2.4 Secure additional base maintenance funds by 2002 to address arduous terrain conditions that adversely impact heavy equipment and other off-road vehicles, restricting capabilities to provide optimum habitat conditions for the panther. (Special Project No. 1)

1.2.5 Evaluate research results from the University of Florida Deer Forage Study. Utilize these and other existing data to amend the Fire Management Plan to guide the frequency, placement, and number of winter versus summer mosaic burns. Use prescribed fire to achieve optimum availability and nutritional quality of deer forage by the year 2002.

1.2.6 Continually monitor and evaluate prey response to the refuge burning program. Implement additional research as needed to fill data gaps. Utilize results to amend the Fire Management Plan.

1.2.7 Refine food plot management for deer. Reestablish experimental food plots based on existing data. Continue to evaluate the nutritional significance of food plots through the use of radio-instrumented deer and other measurements. Evaluate data by the year 2003, and amend the food plot management program as deemed appropriate.

1.2.8 Implement cabbage palm management to restore/ enhance forage composition and growth for deer and other wildlife. Experimental sites where cabbage palm encroachment is documented will be evaluated pre- and post-palm removal to determine forage nutrient benefits for deer by the year 2005. Utilize results to guide further restoration of areas containing heavy cabbage palm infestations.

1.3 Identify and characterize panther responses to habitat management and human activities. Hire a GIS specialist to work on panther issues as well as southwest Florida watershed analysis. (Special Project No. 3)

1.3.1 Continue to monitor panthers, relying primarily on Florida Game and Fresh Water Fish Commission data. Explore the availability/development of effective methods to monitor panthers over a 24-hour period.

1.3.2 Expand information on panther prey activities using telemetry or other methods through the year 2000. In addition, expand data on panther den use, activity patterns, and habitat use.

1.3.3 Have GIS specialist in place by 2002 to digitize panther movements and habitat types in regard to management activities on the refuge.

1.3.4 By 2004, compile regional GIS data on panther responses to habitat management and human activities. Share research findings with other agencies and the public.

1.3.5 Develop GIS data information layers for southwest Florida. Analyze and use data to evaluate and support management decisions by 2004.

1.4 Implement management techniques to enhance other threatened and endangered species.

1.4.1 Construct a greenhouse, with sterile flasking facility, on the refuge and fund the propagation and reintroduction of orchids to the refuge and other depleted habitats by 2001. (Special Project No. 4)

1.4.2 Construct and erect within suitable refuge habitats a minimum of 10 nesting boxes for Big Cypress fox squirrels by 2001.

1.4.3 Develop a plan by the year 2001 that addresses the management of water levels of I-75 canals and the refuge for wood storks and other wading birds. Implement the plan, with concurrence from the Department of Transportation, the South Florida Water Management District, and the Department of Environmental Protection by the year 2005.

1.4.4 Improve feeding areas for wading birds near nest and roost habitat. Using approved mechanical means and herbicides, restore and enhance wetlands as foraging habitat for wading birds in Lucky Lake Strand by 2002. Other potential sites on the refuge will be identified and enhancement activities implemented by 2005.

1.4.5 Continue to utilize the refuge as a reintroduction site for eastern indigo snakes acquired through rehabilitation and confiscations. By the year 2002, establish and implement a protocol to radio-instrument selected specimens for monitoring habitat use, dispersal and survival. By 2009, evaluate results of data to determine the feasibility of the refuge as a repository for this species.

1.4.6 Determine the feasibility of reintroducing red-cockaded woodpeckers to suitable refuge habitats by the year 2004, including evaluation of using Naples stock sources. If feasible, reestablish three colonies on the refuge by the year 2008.

2.0   Restore and conserve the natural diversity, abundance, and ecological function of refuge flora and fauna.

2.1   Minimize the impact from oil and gas exploration and extraction on the refuge.

2.1.1 Explore the potential of acquiring mineral rights on the refuge.

2.1.2 Carefully review oil exploration plans to ensure that adverse impacts to refuge natural and cultural resources are minimized. Refuge staff must ensure the plan employs Best Management Practices. Oil and gas extraction, seismic work, and associated construction will be conducted in a manner that minimizes impacts to wildlife and other refuge resources.

2.1.3 Hire a temporary biologist to accompany seismic work crews and monitor oil well road installation to minimize adverse impacts.

2.1.4 Mitigate for direct and indirect exploration impacts to refuge fauna and habitats through restoration projects.

2.2   Fully develop and implement a prescribed fire program to restore and maintain healthy fire dependent communities by the year 2002.

2.2.1 Implement the 1998 Fire Management Plan, with annual reviews and updates to incorporate applied research findings.

2.2.2 Continue fire research on the effects of burning frequency, seasonality, and spatial distribution on the refuge's pine flatwood, mixed cypress, and wet prairie systems. Produce at least 2 peer-reviewed scientific papers on applied fire ecology by 2005.

2.2.3 Develop fire prescriptions and techniques to enhance prairie orchids and protect the fire sensitive epiphytic orchids.

2.2.4 Obtain funding by the year 2000 to investigate the influence of prescribed fire on the growth and fruiting of saw palmetto (**Senora repens**). Evaluate findings and amend the Fire Management Plan, if deemed appropriate, by the year 2004. (Special Project No. 5)

2.2.5 Obtain funding to investigate the impacts of prescribed fire on reptile populations through the use of radio-telemetry or other methods by the year 2008. (Special Project No. 6)

2.3   Initiate the restoration of at least two native plant communities by the year 2005.

2.3.1 Develop a refuge Habitat Management Plan that incorporates the following key restoration and management strategies by 2003.

   2.3.1.1 Restore a 513-acre fallow farm field in Fire Compartments 44 and 42 that was clear-cut prior to refuge establishment. Plant cypress, maple, etc., in scattered domes to enhance edge habitat and provide potential browse to benefit deer and other wildlife.

   2.3.1.2 Restore a 40-acre fallow farm field in Fire Compartment 12 that was clear-cut prior to refuge establishment. Plant cypress, maple, etc., in scattered domes to enhance edge habitat and provide potential browse to benefit deer and other wildlife.

   2.3.1.3 Restore approximately 800 acres in cooperation with the South Florida Water Management District, partially restore the winter hydroperiod to Lucky Lake and Stumpy strands with the installation of a water control structure in Merritt Canal by 2000. This action will reduce the spread of invasive exotic and drier successional plant species that are invading the strands and reinvigorate historic wetland plant species for the benefit of wading birds and other wildlife.

2.4 Develop control and eradication programs for invasive exotic species by the year 2003 and implement segments as identified in the following strategies. (Special Project No. 7)

   2.4.1 By 2000, identify the most problematic species and areas of infestation. For plant species, apply mechanical and herbicide techniques to these areas first.

   2.4.2 By 2002, identify the most effective herbicide type, application, dosage, and season of use for refuge problematic plant species.

   2.4.3 Work with neighbors, public and private, to control exotic seed sources that threaten the refuge. Develop cooperative initiatives by 2003 to address problem areas.

   2.4.4 Develop and implement a control program for invasive exotic fish, reptiles, and amphibians by 2003.

   2.4.5 Continue to host and coordinate an annual southwest Florida Invasive Exotic Plant Workshop for area land managers. The workshop will focus on new invaders to the area, control techniques, opportunities for control equipment and labor cooperation, and other exotic plant issues.

2.5 Implement management techniques to enhance other refuge endemic fauna.

   2.5.1 Restore a 50- 100-acre disturbed site adjacent to SR 29 as a moist soil management area. The area would be managed for waterfowl, wading birds, and shorebirds by water level management and tilling practices. (Special Project No. 12)

   2.5.2 Develop littoral zones and restore native vegetation along pond edges at the Colding and Pistol ponds to enhance habitat for fish, birds, and other fauna.

2.5.3 Develop and implement a nesting box program for wood ducks and prothonotary warblers.

2.5.4 Determine the distribution and population status of the Big Cypress fox squirrel, Everglades mink, Florida grasshopper sparrow, eastern indigo snake, long-tailed weasel, and other declining species by the year 2007. Incorporate the information into the GIS and implement management actions as deemed appropriate.

2.5.5 Contract biologists to census populations of amphibians and invertebrates to determine baseline levels and trends by the year 2008. (Special Project No. 8)

2.6 Evaluate and monitor hydrologic conditions on the refuge for developing and implementing strategies to restore and maintain healthy water regimes.

2.6.1 Collaborate with the South Florida Water Management District to complete the Lucky Lake Strand project to restore the hydrologic regime to the west side of the refuge.

2.6.2 Recruit a hydrologist by 2001 to compile historic data, assess current water quality and quantity parameters, determine the refuge water budget, and analyze the watershed needs of the refuge complex. (Special Project No. 9)

2.6.3 Develop and implement a hydrologic monitoring program to assess surface and ground water levels, surface flow, hydroperiod, and quality.

2.6.4 Establish and implement a water management strategy for the refuge by 2004.

3.0 Develop and implement an educational program that will provide an understanding and appreciation of the Florida panther, fish and wildlife ecology, and human influence on ecosystems of south Florida.

3.1 Develop facilities and associated amenities to promote public education of the ecosystem, the panther, and the refuge program by the year 2007.

3.1.1 Partnership with others in the development of a multi-agency visitor and environmental education center at the southwest corner of the SR-29 and I-75 interchange. Develop high quality, conventional exhibits and progressive interactive media displays to feature South Florida Ecosystem management, agency restoration activities, and visitor use opportunities. The center will provide an outdoor classroom in the Big Cypress Watershed for students in Collier County and south Florida. (Special Project No. 10)

3.2. Increase local awareness of the South Florida Ecosystem, the refuge, and the panther through the development and implementation of an outreach program by 2003.

3.2.1 Add three new personnel to the Florida Panther refuge complex staff. These include: 1) Media specialist to coordinate news events, press releases, and information transfer to local, state, and national news outlets (Special Project No. 13); 2) Public use specialist stationed at the refuge to coordinate activities at the I-75 visitor center, refuge interpretive displays, school outreach, and refuge volunteer activities; and 3) Administrative assistant to help process and coordinate the added functions of this initiative. (Special Project No. 10)

3.2.2 Encourage the growth of the "Friends of the Panther Refuge" support group (target of 100 members by 2000). Promote quarterly introspective evaluations of the effectiveness of the group's support efforts. The group will assist with education programs on and off the refuge.

3.2.3 Collaborate with various support groups: i.e., Conservancy of Southwest Florida, State of Florida agencies, National Park Service, Natural Resource Conservation Service, Southwest Florida Environmental Coalition, Native Plant Society, Audubon Society, Sierra Club etc., to support refuge outreach activities. Participate in at least 2 events (National Wildlife Refuge Week, International Migratory Bird Day, Earth Day, etc.) per year.

3.2.4 Develop at least 3 refuge specific lesson plans for local school teachers and community organizations for outreach programs. Subjects to include the panther, refuge management, South Florida Ecosystem issues and restoration efforts.

3.2.5 By 2000, develop teacher workshop material (lesson plans) and host an annual teacher workshop for various school districts.

4.0 Promote interagency and private landowner cooperation for the management of natural and cultural resources within the Big Cypress Watershed.

4.1 Increase communication and share knowledge on land use management techniques with adjacent managers, landowners and the public.

4.1.1 Coordinate and host an annual seminar for southwest Florida land managers (private and public) on habitat management, current research and monitoring, and watershed issues.

4.1.2 Initiate a periodic newsletter on panther/habitat management.

4.1.3 Expand Internet Web Page for the refuge, panther management, and current issues by 1999.

4.1.4 Create a citizen's group of interested parties to promote private and governmental cooperation for the management of the refuge by 1999.

4.2 Establish and maintain written agreements with cooperators that will lead to better management of the ecosystem.

4.2.1 Initiate a conservation easement/lease program to protect critical panther habitat identified in the 1993 Panther Habitat Protection Plan. The variable term easements would apply only to willing participants.

4.2.2 Participate in multi-agency mitigation banks to protect panther habitat. These land banks provide for the restoration and protection of key panther habitat. The refuge would coordinate the formation of these banks and manage the land after restoration has been completed.

4.3 Inform and assist private landowners with federal cooperative programs that will enhance or protect wildlife habitat.

4.3.1 Recruit a private lands biologist in 1998 to coordinate the program.

4.3.2 Start an outreach effort to inform landowners of the variety of federal and state programs available including, but not limited to, "Partners For Wildlife," "Wetland Reserve Program," "Conservation Reserve Program," and "Forest Stewardship Program."

4.4 Facilitate partnerships to manage cultural resources with the National Park Service, the State Historic Preservation Office, professional archaeologists, Native American communities, and the general public.

4.4.1 Procure from the National Park Service copies of reports describing archaeological, anthropological, and historical investigations at Everglades National Park and Big Cypress National Preserve. (Regional Archaeologist)

4.4.2 Enter into a Memorandum of Understanding with the National Park Service and Florida Department of Environmental Protection to enhance law enforcement of the Archaeological Resources Protection Act, the Native American Grave Protection and Repatriation Act, and Section 50 of the Code of Federal Regulations as well as to facilitate investigations of the Archaeological Resources Protection Act violations and unpermitted artifact collection on the refuge. (Regional Archaeologist)

4.4.3 Approach the Miccosukee and Seminole nations for information on and input into the management of significant cultural and sacred sites located within the refuge. (Regional Archaeologist)

4.4.4 Work with local Native American communities to develop an education program regarding their cultural heritage. (Regional Archaeologist)

4.4.5 Identify potential avenues of archaeological and historic investigations and promote interdisciplinary research such as the Southwest Florida Project directed by Dr. Marquardt of the University of Florida, Gainesville. (Regional Archaeologist)

4.4.6 Negotiate an agreement with the Florida State Museum or other appropriate facilities for the permanent curation of archaeological collections and associated documentation derived from archaeological investigations on the refuge. (Regional Archaeologist)

4.4.7 Work with the State Historic Preservation Office to ensure confidentiality of cultural resource data within the refuge and the State of Florida. (Regional Archaeologist)

5.0 Protect refuge cultural resources in accordance with federal and state historic preservation legislation and regulations.

5.1 Conduct a refuge-wide archaeological survey by the year 2005.

5.1.1 Develop a scope of work for a comprehensive archaeological survey of the refuge, a cost estimate, and ranking factors for contractor selection by December 1998 (Regional Archaeologist). Secure funding by 2001.

5.1.2 Develop and implement a plan to protect identified sites in consultation with federally recognized Native American nations, the State Historic Preservation Office, and the professional archaeological community.

5.1.3 Develop a GIS layer for the refuge's archaeological and historic sites. The archaeological/historic layer will mesh with such existing layers for habitat type, vegetative cover, hydrology, and soils being developed by the refuge staff. Layer parameters will be defined by 1999. (Regional Archaeologist)

5.1.4 Work with the State Historic Preservation Office to formally establish which refuge management actions are considered "undertakings" requiring its review and comment by 1999. (Regional Archaeologist)

5.1.5 By 2000, compile a comprehensive literature review of past archaeological, anthropological, and historical investigations within and near the refuge. Produce an annotated bibliography to document the region's history and the utility of the scientific methodology. (Regional Archaeologist)

5.1.6 By 2000, all refuge law enforcement officers will have taken the Archaeological Resources Protection Act training course.

5.2 Determine the significance of known cultural resources.

5.2.1 Determine site limits, chronology, and the integrity of archaeological deposits. (Regional Archaeologist)

5.2.2 The Regional Archaeologist, consulting with the State Historic Preservation Office and the Keeper's Office, will determine each site's eligibility for listing on the National Register of Historic Places.

6.0 Provide opportunities for compatible public use in accordance with the National Wildlife Refuge System Improvement Act of 1997.

6.1 Develop an interpretive trail to allow access and enhance public understanding of the panther and the refuge by the year 2002. (Special Project No. 11)

6.1.1 Construct a 3/4-mile interpretive foot trail in association with the proposed visitor center at the I-75/Highway 29 interchange. The trail will utilize low-impact design, be self-guiding, and feature interpretive signs.

6.1.2 Utilize partnerships (Friends of the Panther Refuge and others) to fund, construct, and maintain the trail, interpretive exhibits and associated facilities.

6.2 Develop a wildlife viewing area for the moist-soil management area located adjacent to SR 29. Facilities will include a gravel parking area, bathroom, viewing platforms, and interpretive signs. (Special Project No. 12)

6.3 Determine compatibility and feasibility of a hunting program on the refuge by accomplishing the following sequential strategies.

6.3.1 Inventory refuge deer and feral hog populations in order to establish baseline indices. Implement techniques developed from a current University of Florida study to index deer abundance and conduct hog monitoring surveys by the year 2000.

6.3.2 Utilize existing panther and hunting data, information from the current University of Tennessee study, and 24-hour activity monitoring studies to evaluate potential impacts of hunting on the panther and prey resources. (Special Project No. 14)

6.3.3 Evaluate potential impacts of hunting on other refuge activities and programs (research, management, maintenance, public use, etc.). (Special Project No. 15)

6.3.4 Evaluate potential impacts that "hunt administration" could have on other refuge programs (competition for manpower, equipment, funding, etc).

6.3.5 Evaluate hunter access issues (access limitations, potential impacts to roads/trails, etc.).

6.3.6 Determine if hunting would be considered compatible with the primary purpose for which the refuge was established.

6.3.7 Determine if hunting on the refuge would be in the public interest.

6.4 Determine compatibility and feasibility of fishing at two sites on the refuge.

6.4.1 By 2000, determine the mercury level of fish in Pistol and Colding ponds by enlisting the cooperation of the Service's Ecological Services Division on sampling and contaminants analysis. (Special Project No. 16)

6.4.2 Inventory fishery resources in Pistol and Colding ponds by employing electro shocking techniques through cooperation of the Service's Fisheries Division.

6.4.3 Evaluate the costs, logistics, and safety considerations in creating suitable sites for fishing in Pistol and Colding ponds. The evaluation will consider options of partnership assistance to defray costs and/or gain assistance for site development. (Special Project No. 17)

Plan Implementation

The future of this refuge, like most national wildlife refuges, is dependent upon a public constituency that is knowledgeable of refuge resources and mandates, as well as environmental issues, and is willing to work towards resolving them. The expanded educational, recreational, and partnership opportunities proposed in this plan will help build and maintain this needed constituency. Promoting the refuge as a natural and recreational asset of Collier County will enhance the refuge's image and help expand local support.

Partnerships

Implementation of this plan will rely on partnerships formed with landowners in the watershed, volunteers and interested citizens, farm and conservation organizations, and with appropriate government agencies. Cooperating landowners within the refuge watershed would be offered incentives and/or compensated through cost-sharing agreements for applying conservation and environmental farming practices and for creating, maintaining, or enhancing habitat for wildlife. Annual management workshops and periodic newsletters will enhance the cooperative management within the Big Cypress Watershed.

Little blue heron
USFWS photo by Larry W. Richardson

Annual Work Plans

Future annual work plans will be written to reflect the priorities and intent of the plan. When discretionary funding and staff resources are available, they will be used to implement components of the plan.

Step-Down Plans

The plan provides conceptual guidance for potential future expansion, management, and development of the refuge. Before implementing the strategies and projects, additional step-down plans will need to be prepared. These range from habitat management and site development plans to updating the fire management plan. Refuge staff will look for innovative partnerships with local professional and business groups to assist in preparing and implementing detailed step-down plans.

This list of step-down plans for the refuge include:

Plan Required	Completion Date
Fire Management Plan	FY98
Habitat Management Plan	FY01
Refuge Visitor Services/Interpretive Plan	FY01

Green-backed heron
USFWS Photo by Nick Milam

The refuge was allocated $747,000 in FY 1997. The fire program represents almost 40 percent of the dollars allocated to the refuge. Without this program, the refuge could not function because general operating funds are not keeping up with staff and basic operating costs of the refuge.

The increased funding required by this plan will come through a variety of internal and external sources. New projects will be identified in the Refuge Operating Needs System (RONS). The refuge staff will look for ways of leveraging and matching dollars through new and innovative sources (both public and private). The full implementation of this plan will be dependent on Congressional allocations and new sources of funding as a result of partnerships and grants.

The following summary provides a list of refuge projects:

Project 1. Additional Base Maintenance Funds
Additional base funding is needed to address the arduous terrain conditions of the refuge that adversely impact equipment and vehicles. Habitat management, research, biological monitoring, law enforcement, and public access depend upon the successful maintenance of: 4 swamp buggies, 5 all-terrain vehicles, 2 tractors, 1 dozer, 1 dozer transport, 1 dump truck, 1 front-end loader, and numerous assorted 2 and 4 wheel drive vehicles. In addition, this station maintains 1 air boat and 3 boats (18-22 ft.) with 80-200 horsepower outboards for Ten Thousand Islands National Wildlife Refuge. Three new staff positions are needed for this project. An automotive mechanic to maintain and repair engines on the various pieces of equipment and a maintenance worker to address the minor repairs and scheduled maintenance needs of the equipment. The additional maintenance, biological, and management programs would also require the recruitment of an assistant refuge manager to manage and facilitate program management. This assistant would be shared with Ten Thousand Islands refuge. The estimated cost for these three full-time employees is approximately $300,000 per year including employee benefits. In addition, $100,000 is needed in base maintenance funds to address equipment breakdowns, scheduled maintenance, and preventive maintenance needs.

Project 2. Roger Roth Work Center Rehabilitation
Equipment storage and maintenance support facilities are performed out of an old house containing a rotting, wooden frame which presents unsafe conditions for staff and visitors. The Service will contract out ($200,000) for the construction of 2 metal buildings, 25'x30', for logistical support and facilitation of maintenance operations and equipment storage. Part of the project would include the construction of new bathroom facilities and septic system to accommodate staff additions. Approximately $30,000 is needed for annual maintenance needs for the work center.

Night-scented orchid
USFWS photo by Larry W. Richardson

Project 3. Enhance Habitat Assessment through Geographic Information System Analysis

To meet the refuge goal of assessing panther responses to habitat management and watershed analysis, a GIS specialist is needed. This person would digitize panther movements and habitat types on and off the refuge. This person would assist other staff members and cooperating agencies with their GIS needs. New hardware would also be required including digitizing equipment, computer, printer and plotter. The estimated hardware costs are $100,000, and the estimated cost of the GIS specialist is $100,000 including employee benefits.

Project 4. Rare Orchid Restoration Project

Over 46 species of orchids have been documented in the Fakahatchee Strand. These plants contribute in making southwest Florida a truly unique natural environment. Many of these orchids have been pilfered by humans and are now rare. Through a combination agency and organization partnership, this project would restore rare orchid species to suitable, historic habitats in southwest Florida. Cooperating land management entities include: Florida Panther National Wildlife Refuge, Big Cypress National Preserve, Fakahatchee Strand State Preserve, Picayune Strand State Forest, CREW lands, and National Audubon Society's Corkscrew Sanctuary. The project is supported by state and federal agencies, Florida Native Plant Society, and the Florida Orchid Society. The project would focus on the creation of a small greenhouse at the refuge where orchids would be grown for eventual transplantation. Land managers would

Cigar orchid
USFWS photo by Larry W. Richardson

provide seed pods from a select list of rare orchids. The seeds would be flasked by an orchid grower and grown at the refuge greenhouse until ready for transplantation to selected native habitats. The plants would be mapped using GPS technology and monitored for health and survival. One-time funding of $20,000 is needed for the greenhouse building and equipment costs. In addition, recurring funding ($20,000) for a temporary greenhouse caretaker is needed.

Prescribed burn at Florida Panther Refuge
USFWS photo by Larry W. Richardson

Project 5. Research Project on the Effects of Prescribed Fire on Saw Palmetto
The saw palmetto is a very important plant for wildlife in south Florida. Not only does its fruit provide food for a multitude of animals, but the dense thickets of this plant provide resting and denning cover for panthers. Research is needed to determine the effects of fire on this plants growth and fruit production. Research results would be helpful to refuge managers as well as other land managers in south Florida. The study would be under contract to a university or the federal biological research division for 3 years at $50,000/year. The end products would result in management recommendations to benefit the panther, and a peer-reviewed paper in a biological periodical.

Project 6. Research Project on the Effects of Prescribed Fire on Reptile Populations
The refuge contains a large reptile population. One endangered species, the eastern indigo snake, is present on the refuge. Prescribed fire effects on reptile populations is not well known. Basic research is needed to evaluate how prescribe burning parameters such as season, ignition methods, and burn rotation affects refuge reptiles. Research results would help refuge managers and other land managers in south Florida. The study would be under contract to a university or the federal biological research division for 3 years at $50,000/year. The end product would result in management recommendations to benefit reptiles on the refuge, and a peer-reviewed paper in a biological periodical.

Project 7. Invasive Exotic Plant Species Control
Invasive exotic plants are a major threat to the native plant communities of south Florida. Brazilian pepper, melaleuca, cogon grass and climbing fern are the refuge problem species. This project will help stop the encroachment of these invasive plants by supporting a control program containing the following elements: the acquisition of a 4-wheel drive, 75hp

tractor ($60,000) to pull a herbicide spray rig; the initiation of a seasonal plant control crew consisting of 2 seasonal workers ($20,000); maintenance funds for spray equipment and personnel safety ($10,000); and $5,000 for herbicide costs. In addition, $3,000 per year is needed for Service sponsorship of an annual Invasive Exotic Plant Workshop. The Workshop would provide a forum where state, federal, and private land managers of southwest Florida could meet and discuss problem plants, successful control techniques, equipment and project partnerships, and network on the invasive exotic plant problem. The estimated cost for this project is $88,000, with recurring costs of $38,000/year.

Eastern indigo snake

Project 8. Baseline Populations of Amphibians and Invertebrates
Knowledge on the animal diversity of an area is critical to habitat management assessment and planning. These are the last of the animal groups that have yet to be inventoried on the refuge. The plan proposes to temporarily hire or contract out the inventory of these animals to determine baseline levels. Data collection would include species lists and a reference study collection which would take place over a period of a year for each group. The estimated cost for these surveys is $30,000.

Project 9. Recruit a Hydrologist to Analyze Watershed Needs
It is clearly evident, as a result of information received during the planning process, that watershed protection and a coordinated watershed management effort is needed to protect the natural resources of southwest Florida. The two Service refuges in Collier County are located within the Big Cypress Watershed and are intimately involved in all planning that will occur within the watershed. A hydrologist is needed to fully assess the impacts of various surface projects planned on and off the refuge within the watershed. One planned project is the re-hydration of the South Golden Gate Estates, which will effect both refuges. The hydrologist would also provide information to adjacent land managers, as well as county, state, and federal land planning efforts for south Florida. This position would be shared with Ten Thousand Islands refuge. The estimated cost for this position is $100,000/year including employee benefits.

Project 10. Develop Education Facilities
As information from the public clearly pointed out during the planning process, the key to success will be public education and support of refuge programs and the panther recovery effort. The Service has no education/ interpretation facilities in Collier County aside from a temporary display placed in the Southwest Florida Environmental Information Center. Two sites are planned for refuge exhibits and environmental information materials. One site will be located adjacent to the Florida Panther refuge on Florida Department of Environmental Protection lands at the intersection of highways I-75 and SR29. At this location, a multi-agency visitor center is planned that will display the various land management programs and restoration efforts underway for south Florida. The Service will need an estimated $100,000 to create 4-8 exhibits. The site could also serve as an environmental education center for the youth of Collier County. Its central location between Everglades City, Naples, and Immokalee, as well as access to the Big Cypress Swamp, offers an ideal location for this venture. Another $100,000 is estimated as the Service's share needed for the building and educational materials. The second site is at the Southwest Florida Environmental Information Center adjacent to Ten Thousand Islands refuge and Port of the Islands Hotel. An estimated $20,000 is needed to fund 4 exhibits that would include information on Florida Panther refuge and the panther recovery effort. A public use specialist would be recruited to plan, maintain, and coordinate staffing of the centers, as well as coordinate volunteer activities on the refuge. The extra administrative duties would also require an additional clerical position for the refuge. These two positions would cost an estimated $175,000/year with employee benefits.

Project 11. Develop an Interpretive Foot Trail

Through a combination of volunteer partnerships, multi-agency coordination, and cost-share funding opportunities, construct a 1/2-3/4 mile interpretive foot trail on the refuge. The trail would be located in the southeast corner of the refuge where limited panther activity has occurred. The trail would also be accessed from the proposed I-75 Visitor Center. The trail would feature low-impact design and self-guiding interpretive exhibits that would enhance public understanding of the panther and refuge programs. Portions of the trail that are wet would have boardwalks constructed over them. A gravel parking area and vault bathroom facilities would be constructed at the trail head. The estimated cost of this project is $40,000 with $10,000/year maintenance costs after the first year.

Project 12. Develop Waterbird Habitat and a Wildlife Viewing Area

On the east side of the refuge, adjacent to SR29, lies a 400-acre disturbed area that was farmed prior to refuge establishment. The cypress and other mixed swamp tree species were cut to accommodate these farm fields. This area now is a mixture of wetland grasses and shrub. This project proposes to manage approximately 50-100 acres of the area as moist-soil impoundments. Three or four cell units surrounding a hardwood hammock would be managed at different water levels to benefit migrating and resident waterfowl, wading birds, and shorebirds. The area would be accessible to the public to view the birds and the successful management operation. Collier County has limited opportunities for safe wildlife viewing and such an area would be a tremendous asset for southwest Florida. Because the area is so wet, it has limited use by panthers. Initial costs include the restoration of farm field levees ($30,000), water pumping facilities ($80,000), construction of parking area ($25,000), vault bathroom ($12,000), and interpretive signs ($15,000). The project would require recurring maintenance costs of $20,000/year.

Project 13. Initiate a Panther and Ecosystem Outreach Program

Educating the public about refuge management, the plight of the panther, and recovery efforts clearly is the key to a successful program. To implement such a program will require a coordinated, cooperative effort between federal, state, and private entities. The Service proposes to enhance the refuge program by adding a media specialist to keep the news outlets informed of current and planned events. In addition, the public use specialist identified in Project 10 would develop and distribute panther information to school program coordinators. The media specialist is estimated to cost $100,000/year including employee benefits and will be a shared position with Ten Thousand Islands refuge.

Project 14. Research Project - Potential Impacts of Hunting on Panthers/24-Hour Activity Monitoring

More information is needed in order to make a compatibility determination on whether hunting should be permitted on Florida Panther refuge. This study would follow the same design as the current study by Professor Joe Clark of the University of Tennessee, however, the data would be gathered on panthers over a 24-hour activity period. GPS satellite telemetry would have to be employed or another technology designed to gather the same information. The refuge would again serve as a control site where hunting does not occur. Research results would help refuge managers and other land managers in south Florida to make compatibility determinations on hunting. The study would be under contract to a university or the federal biological research division for 3 years at $50,000/year. The end product would be a peer-reviewed paper in a biological periodical.

Snowy egret with young
USFWS Photo by David Hall

Snowy egrets and Glossy ibis
USFWS Photo by Diane Borden-Billiot

Project 15. Research Project - Potential Impacts of Hunting on Other Refuge Programs
This study would also help management make a compatibility determination on hunting for Florida Panther refuge. Data obtained from Project 15 would be evaluated by refuge biologists in conjunction with ongoing and planned research to determine if hunting activity may have an adverse impact on refuge programs. The project would be undertaken with existing resources and would not require additional funding resources.

Project 17. Research Project - Determine the Mercury Levels of Fish in Pistol and Colding Ponds
Past fish collections from Pistol and Colding ponds have indicated varying mercury levels, but all were high and some records exceeded human consumption standards. To better understand the contamination level, more sampling is prudent. This will be a cooperative effort requiring fishery assistance (electro-shock boat) from either a state or federal agency. In addition, $6,000-10,000 is needed to run the mercury tests.

Project 18. Evaluate the Safety and Feasibility of a Fishing Program for Colding and Pistol Ponds
This study would also help management make a compatibility determination on fishing on Florida Panther refuge. Colding and Pistol ponds are not natural lakes. They are actually pits created after fill material was excavated for SR29. The banks are not gradual, but steep sided, with nearly a vertical drop of 10-15 feet around the entire bank. This presents an extremely hazardous bank fishing situation, especially if small children were involved. To remedy this hazard the bank slope would have to be cut or filled. Another measure may include the construction of a fishing pier. In addition, the existing fishery is extremely limited, thus the reason for the shock boat requirement in Project 17. Refuge staff will assess these various factors and determine if a fishing program is compatible and worth the expense of initiating the program. No additional costs will be incurred with this evaluation project.

Figure 11. Project Cost Summary

Projects	One Time Cost	First-Year Need	Recurring Base
1. Add Base Maintenance Funds	$200,000	$400,000	$400,000
2. Replace Work Center Buildings	100,000	230,000	30,000
3. GIS Specialist	20,000	200,000	100,000
4. Orchid Restoration Project	150,000	40,000	20,000
5. Prescribed Fire/Saw Palmetto	150,000	150,000	
6. Prescribed Fire/Reptiles	150,000	150,000	
7. Exotic Plant Species Control	50,000	88,000	38,000
8. Amphibians and Invertebrates	30,000	30,000	
9. Hydrologist/Watershed Needs		100,000	100,000
10. Develop Education Facilities	220,000	395,000	175,000
11. Interpretive Foot Trail	40,000	50,000	10,000
12. Waterbird Habitat / Viewing Area	172,000	192,000	20,000
13. Outreach Program		100,000	100,000
14. Panthers/24-Hour Monitoring	150,000	150,000	
15. Impacts of Hunting on Programs	0	0	
16. Mercury Levels in Ponds	10,000	10,000	
17. Feasibility of Fishing Program	0	0	
TOTALS	$1,442,000	$2,285,000	$993,000

Volunteers

Volunteer assistance to the refuge grew appreciably during the last two years due to substantial contributions of the AmeriCorps volunteers and to various individuals working on biological projects. Not considering AmeriCorps assistance, a total of 51 volunteers contributed 1865 hours in three major areas in 1996; i.e., resource management, administration, and public use support. Most assistance was gained in wildlife monitoring.

Volunteers will continue to play a critical role in assisting staff with fulfilling the future vision of the refuge. In addition, while not required of all those who participate in the group "Friends of the Panther Refuge," many of these interested citizens will be enlisted as volunteers to perform various refuge activities.

Staff

A staff of thirteen permanent and six temporary/seasonal positions has been approved for the Florida Panther National Wildlife Refuge Complex. Nine additional positions are proposed to work specifically on implementing the refuge comprehensive conservation plan. Five of these positions will be shared with Ten Thousand Islands National Wildlife Refuge. These include an easement biologist, auto mechanic, maintenance worker, public use specialist, administrative assistant (shared), GIS specialist (shared), hydrologist (shared), assistant refuge manager (shared), and a media specialist (shared). Figure 12 displays the organizational diagram for the future management of Florida Panther and Ten Thousand Islands refuges.

Monitoring and Evaluation

Extensive research and monitoring of natural resources have always been a major part of the management of the refuge. Some of the studies target the collection of baseline data on the environmental parameters of the area. This knowledge will give managers a data base on which to judge how habitat management, changes in water quantity and quality, or other environmental changes have impacted refuge resources. A major objective of research studies is that the products will benefit not only the refuge but other land managers as well. Most research has centered on panthers, deer, and the effects of the prescribed burning program on habitat and wildlife.

The plan will be augmented by detailed step-down management plans to address management actions in support of refuge goals and objectives and to implement the identified strategies. Every five years the plan will be revisited to document progress and reassess direction. Public involvement in evaluating progress and plan implementation will be encouraged.

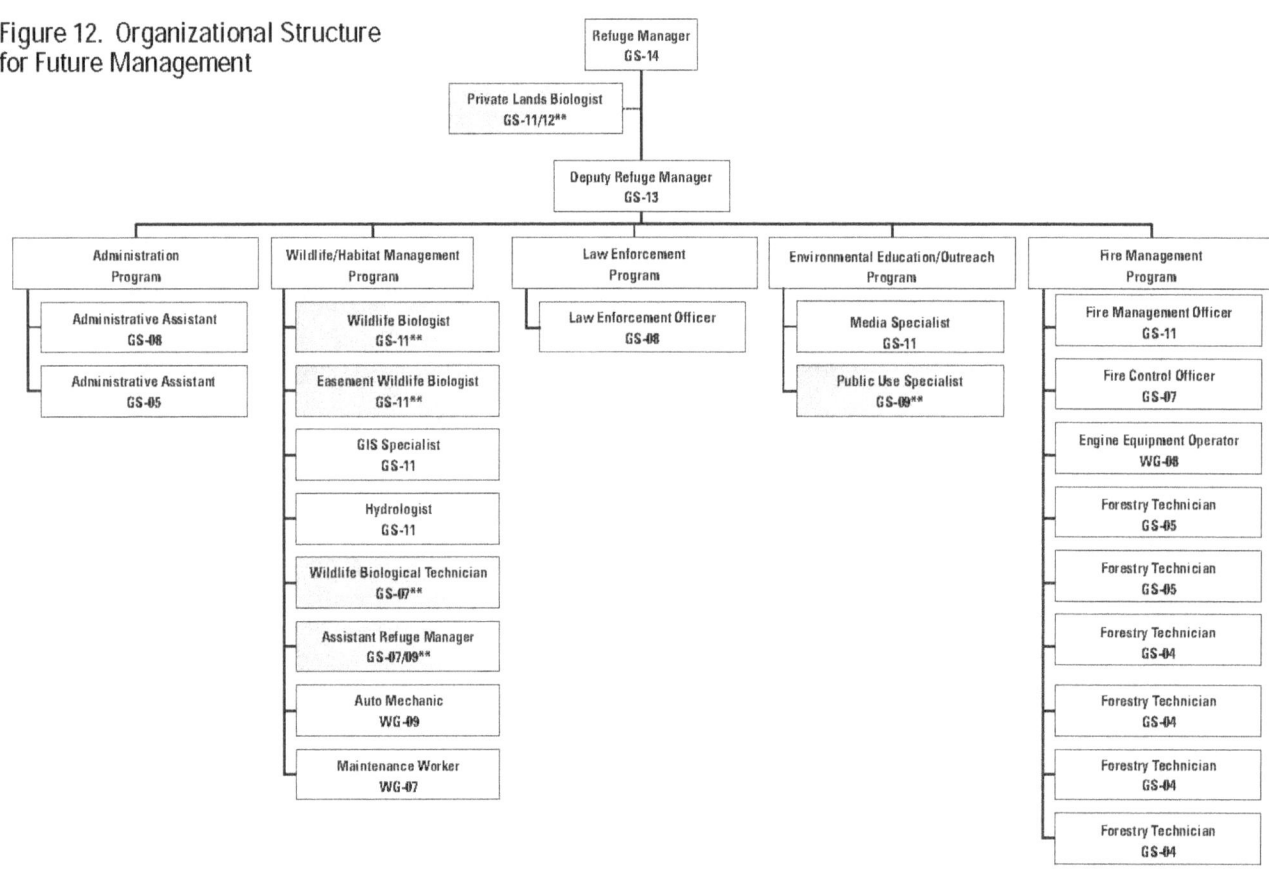

Figure 12. Organizational Structure for Future Management

Note
(**) Indicates positions filled exclusively for Florida Panther National Wildlife Refuge and/or Refuge Easement Program. All other positions are shared with Ten Thousand Islands National Wildlife Refuge.

Draft
Finding of No Significant Impact

Florida Panther National Wildlife Refuge
Comprehensive Conservation Plan
Collier County, Florida

The U.S. Fish and Wildlife Service proposes to publicly disclose the possible environmental consequences that implementation of the Florida Panther National Wildlife Refuge Comprehensive Conservation Plan could have on the quality of the physical, biological, and human environment, as required by the National Environmental Policy Act of 1969.

The Service has analyzed the following alternatives to the proposal in an Environmental Assessment.

1). Alternative A (No Action) Advocates the refuge continue to be managed under its current management direction. The refuge has been closed to public access except for limited, small group tours. Essentially, the refuge is managed as inviolate sanctuary for the endangered Florida panther;

2). Alternative B (Ecosystem Approach) Meets the needs of the resources, and allows some access to the public for wildlife observation and environmental education. The Service would also study the compatibility and feasibility of allowing hunting and fishing to occur on the refuge; and,

3). Alternative C (Maximum Public Use Programs on the Refuge) Emphasizes public use and environmental education programs on the refuge. Those activities would be allowed, coupled with research to determine their impact on the endangered Florida panther.

The preferred alternative selected for implementation is **Alternative B**; implement the Florida Panther National Wildlife Refuge Comprehensive Conservation Plan and establish refuge management direction pursuant to the goals, objectives, and strategies contained in the plan. This alternative was selected because it best meets the primary purposes for which the refuge was established--protecting and enhancing panther habitat while maintaining natural diversity. This alternative recognizes the importance of the refuge within the Big Cypress Watershed and defines refuge actions to protect and enhance the natural features of this ecosystem.

Implementation of the agency's decision would be expected to result in the following environmental, social, and economic effects: This alternative will provide the public with limited access to the refuge, which has been a major issue. This access will benefit refuge programs by informing the public about refuge programs, the plight of the panther, and other wildlife that use the refuge. The conservation easement program will facilitate the protection of panther habitats in south Florida and involve only willing private landowners. The program should prove to be a major step in the conservation of critical resources within the South Florida Ecosystem.

Visitation will be monitored for its impacts on flora and fauna of the refuge. Development of new refuge facilities will cause minimal disturbance to refuge lands. It will not adversely impact endangered or threatened species or adversely impact wetlands, neither will it harm nor cause the loss or destruction of archaeological or historical resources. The preferred alternative will restore 40 acres of disturbed wetlands in refuge compartment No. 12; 513 acres of disturbed wetlands within refuge compartment Nos. 42 and 44; 800 acres of wetlands within Lucky Lake and Stumpy strands; and, achieve protection of 370,000 acres of priority panther habitat in southwest Florida. This alternative will have a positive effect on visitor use, environmental education, conservation of natural resources, and local communities.

Measures to mitigate and/or minimize adverse effects have been incorporated into the proposal. Where site development activities will be proposed during the next 15 years, each activity would be given the appropriate NEPA consideration. At that time, any required mitigation activities would be designed into the specific project to reduce any significant adverse impacts to the environment. Long-term monitoring will help in determining actual effects and how the Service should respond.

The proposal is not expected to have any significant adverse effects on wetlands and floodplains, pursuant to Executive Orders 11990 and 11988.

Finding Of No Significant Impact

The preferred alternative has been thoroughly coordinated with all interested and/or affected parties. A list of parties contacted may be found in Appendix C of the Draft Comprehensive Conservation Plan.

Copies of the Environmental Assessment are available by writing:

U.S. Fish and Wildlife Service
1875 Century Boulevard
Atlanta, Georgia 30345

It is my determination that the preferred alternative will not have a significant impact on the human environment in accordance with Section 102 (2)(c) of the National Environmental Policy Act, and in accordance with the Service's Administrative Manual (30 AM.9B(2)(d), and further conclude that an Environmental Impact Statement is not necessary. This determination is based on the following factors (40 CFR 1508.27):

1. Both beneficial and adverse effects have been considered and this action will not have a significant effect on the human environment. (Environmental Assessment, pages 58-61.)

2. The actions will not have a significant effect on public health and safety. (Environmental Assessment, pages 58-61.)

3. The project will not significantly effect any unique characteristics of the geographic area such as proximity to historical or cultural resources, wild and scenic rivers, or ecologically critical areas. (Environmental Assessment, pages 58, 59, and 61.)

4. The effects on the quality of the human environment are not likely to be highly controversial. (Environmental Assessment, page 58.)

5. The actions do not involve highly uncertain, unique, or unknown environmental risks to the human environment. (Environmental Assessment, pages 58-61.)

6. The actions will not establish a precedent for future actions with significant effects nor does it represent a decision in principle about a future consideration. (Environmental Assessment, pages 58-61.)

7. There will be no cumulatively significant impacts on the environment. Cumulative impacts have been analyzed with consideration of other similar activities on adjacent lands, in past action, and in foreseeable future actions. (Environmental Assessment, page 64.)

8. The actions will not significantly affect any site listed in, or eligible for listing in, the National Register of Historic Places, nor will they cause loss or destruction of significant scientific, cultural, or historic resources. (Environmental Assessment, page 61.)

9. The actions are not likely to adversely affect endangered or threatened species, or their habitats. (Environmental Assessment, pages 59-60.)

10. The actions will not lead to a violation of federal, state, or local laws imposed for the protection of the environment. (Environmental Assessment, pages 66-74.)

Supporting References:

Environmental Assessment
Comprehensive Conservation Plan

_____
Sam D. Hamilton
Regional Director

_____
Date

Draft Environmental Assessment

for the Florida Panther
National Wildlife Refuge

U.S. Department of the Interior
Fish and Wildlife Service
Southeast Regional Office
1875 Century Boulevard
Atlanta, Georgia 30345

August 1998

Purpose and Need for Action

Introduction

The U.S. Fish and Wildlife Service proposes to implement a Comprehensive Conservation Plan to guide the management of the Florida Panther National Wildlife Refuge, Collier, County, Florida, over the next ten to fifteen years.

The purpose of this Environmental Assessment is to analyze and evaluate the environmental effects of implementing a proposed alternative management framework for the refuge.

The proposed action is to implement Alternative B: Ecosystem Approach, as described in the Proposed Management Direction of the Draft Comprehensive Conservation Plan.

Formal consultation for this Environmental Assessment did not occur. However, this planning effort and the refuge manager's ongoing dialogue with various federal and state jurisdictions, interest groups, and private landowners, has provided important elements in the synthesis of the proposed goals, objectives, and strategies found in the draft plan. Implementation of the plan will necessitate further coordination and cooperation with these entities.

White-tail deer fawn
Photo by the U.S. Forest Service

Wood storks
Photo by John and Karen Hollingsworth

Alternatives Including Proposed Action

The following alternatives address the major issues regarding Florida Panther National Wildlife Refuge. Each alternative will be analyzed for its appropriateness in meeting the needs of the public and purpose/mission of the refuge. The end result is a set of goals, objectives, and strategies related to each issue which would assist in making management decisions.

Alternative A: No Action

Access:

In this alternative, the plan would advocate that the refuge continue to be managed under its current management direction. The refuge has been closed to public access except for limited, small group tours. Essentially, the refuge is managed as an inviolate sanctuary for the endangered Florida panther.

Due to the sensitive nature of the endangered species associated with the refuge, the environmental education and public use programs would not be expanded, in that no interpretive or recreational trails would not be developed, neither would there be a hunting nor a fishing program. The refuge currently offers access for limited small group tours and outreach opportunities for school groups off the refuge. Instead, this alternative advocates more of an "off-refuge" approach which would still meet interpretive and educational goals.

Cooperative Land Management and Partnerships within the Big Cypress Watershed:

Currently, there are limited partnering opportunities with adjacent landowners and governmental agencies to cooperatively manage the watershed for the protection of hydrologic, ecological, and environmental values of the system.

The manager is a trustee for the Corkscrew Regional Ecosystem Watershed, a 60,000-acre proposed natural area north of the refuge. The manager has also been a member of the State of Florida Big Cypress Basin Ecological Management Area Team and the Big Cypress Basin Project Coordination Team for the South Florida Ecosystem Restoration effort. The manager is also an ex-officio member of the Natural Resources Committee for the University of Florida Institute of Food and Agricultural Sciences in southwest Florida. In addition, the manager serves on the Big Cypress Basin Science Workshop Steering Committee and the oversight committee for ecological monitoring of the proposed hydrologic restoration of the South Golden Gate Estates. Lastly, the manager serves as the chairman of the multi-agency committee to establish an environmental information center at the Port of the Islands.

Public Awareness of the Panther and Refuge Programs:

The refuge would remain closed to public access. Due to the lack of a visitor contact station at the refuge, the public would have limited means of obtaining important information on the panther, its habitat, or refuge programs. Opportunities for increased environmental education would not be promoted, and partnering for better watershed management and habitat conservation would not be pursued.

Protect Panther Habitat on Private Lands:

No incentives would be provided to encourage private landowners to sell their land or maintain important panther habitat beyond the boundaries of the refuge.

Wood storks and Great egrets
USFWS photo by Larry W. Richardson

Refuge Research and Management:
Research projects such as panther monitoring, prescribed fire impacts, and plant, animal and hydrological baseline monitoring exist. Current management practices would continue, but not modified or expanded. Day-to-day operational activities would continue to revolve around intensive field work regarding management of habitats for the panther and other species of concern such as the wood stork. The refuge is currently used as a control site (non-hunting area) for studies that are ongoing and planned in the future to determine the impacts of human activities on the panther.

Routine field work includes monitoring and observing panther activities, ecosystem assessments of water quality issues, prescribed burning, and habitat manipulation to improve deer forage. There would be no public use program.

Lack of Adequate Staff:
The refuge cannot successfully meet its Service or South Florida Ecosystem responsibilities at current staffing levels. These responsibilities go beyond habitat management on the refuge for the panther.

Gas and Oil Exploration:
Most of the refuge's subsurface minerals are not owned by the Government. Surface mineral exploration has not occurred since the refuge was established. However, a plan for seismic work and oil well exploration from Collier interests has been submitted to the refuge. Exploration will have an impact on the resources of the refuge. The Service will review the plan to minimize these impacts.

Supporting Management Goals:
1.0   Provide optimum habitat conditions for the Florida panther with special consideration for other endangered and threatened species.

2.0   Restore and conserve the natural diversity, abundance, and ecological function of refuge flora and fauna.

Alternative B: Ecosystem Approach (Proposed Action)
A description of the Ecosystem Approach may be found in the Draft
Comprehensive Conservation Plan.

American aligator
USFWS photo by Larry W. Richardson

Alternative C: Maximize Public Use Programs on the Refuge

Access:

Maximum public use and environmental education programs would be stepped up considerably. Facilities such as parking lots, paved roads, trails, auto loops, and restrooms would be developed on the refuge to accommodate increased public use. Secondary uses such as hunting, fishing, and camping would also be allowed and coupled with some research to determine if those uses are compatible with the purpose of the refuge. Secondary uses on the refuge would risk inflicting adverse impacts on the panther and/or jeopardizing habitat needs of the panther. Research and monitoring would be minimized because they would conflict with public use management. There would be no need or regard for additional research except for that which would aid management in determining whether to disallow or increase secondary uses and activities on the refuge.

Waterfowl
USFWS photo by Larry W. Richardson

Cooperative Land Management and Partnerships Within Big Cypress Watershed:

Less emphasis than Alternative B will be placed on working with the local community, private landowners, and other jurisdictions. General partnerships on management and cooperation with various watershed entities that would lead to overall land and watershed protection and stewardship of the resources would be pursued. More communication and coordination with the other land managers within the watershed would occur.

Public Awareness of the Panther and Refuge Programs:

Activities designed to educate the public would be limited to on-refuge programs only. Plans to develop a multi-agency visitor center would be pursued.

Protect Panther Habitat on Private Lands:

There would be no efforts to protect the panther on private lands. All management efforts would be focused towards on-refuge activities.

Refuge Research and Management:

Current research practices would continue with the development of some new partnerships for research to benefit refuge management specifically targeting the effects of secondary use activities.

Lack of Adequate Staff:

Additional staff would be needed to enhance the education and outreach program on the refuge.

Gas and Oil Exploration:

Resources would be managed to minimize the adverse impacts of gas and oil exploration on the refuge.

Supporting Management Goals:

4.0   Promote interagency and private landowner cooperation for the management of natural and cultural resources within the Big Cypress Watershed.

6.0   Provide opportunities for compatible public use in accordance with the National Refuge System Improvement Act of 1997.

Figure 13. Issues and Alternatives Matrix

	Alternative A No Action	Alternative B Ecosystem Approach	Alternative C Maximum Public Use
Public Access	Limit to current levels of small group tours	Increase access a) develop interpretive trail b) develop waterbird viewing area	Increase access a) develop interpretive trail b) develop waterbird viewing area c) develop additional hiking with interpretation c) develop additional wildlife viewing areas along I-75 and SR 29
	No hunting or fishing	Study compatibility of hunting and fishing	Study compatibility of hunting and fishing
Outreach	Limited on-refuge and off-refuge activities	Increased education efforts on-refuge and off-refuge	Limited to on-refuge education
	No multi-agency visitor center	Develop multi-agency visitor center	Develop multi-agency visitor center
Cooperative Management and Partnerships	Limited partnering for panther habitat protection, watershed protection, and ecosystem restoration	Develop partnerships to co-op; manage watershed to protect panther habitat, hydrology, ecology, and environmental values of the system	Develop partnerships to protect panther habitat on refuge
	No conservation easement program	Maximum conservation easement program; 10,000 acres adjacent to refuge; 360,000 acres in southwest Florida	No conservation easement program
	Limited off-refuge ecosystem restoration	Develop off-refuge ecosystem restoration projects	Limited off-refuge ecosystem restoration projects
Research and Management	Continue existing research to refine management programs on the refuge	Implement new research and develop new partnerships to continually enhance refuge research projects and management programs on and off the refuge	Continue existing research to refine management programs on refuge
Lack of Adequate Staffing	Maintain current staffing	Increase staffing	Increase staffing
Oil and Gas	Manage resources to help minimize the adverse impacts of gas and oil exploration	Acquire mineral rights to protect refuge surface resources	Manage resources to help minimize the adverse impacts of gas and oil exploration

Florida black bear
USFWS photo by Larry W. Richardson

Affected Environment

The refuge encompasses the northern origin of the Fakahatchee Strand, which is the largest cypress strand in the Big Cypress drainage basin. Orchids and other rare swamp plants grow within the swamp's interior. The refuge contains a diverse mix of pine forests, cypress domes, marl prairies, hardwood hammocks, and lakes surrounded by swamps.

In addition to the panther, 20 other species of animals are found in the refuge vicinity that are either state or federally listed as endangered, threatened, or species of special concern. The Florida black bear, alligator, wood stork, roseate spoonbill, limpkin, eastern indigo snake, Florida grasshopper sparrow, Everglades mink, and Big Cypress fox squirrel are a few examples. Other resident wildlife include whitetail deer and feral hogs, which are important panther prey species. Turkey and bobwhite quail are also found on the refuge.

Climate

The subtropical climate is directly responsible for many of the refuge's features. It is warm enough to permit year-round growth of many forms of plant life and wet enough to replenish the areas of standing water during the rainy season. Temperatures occasionally fall below freezing in winter and rise above 90°F during the summer with an average annual temperature of about 73°F.

Physiography and Hydrology

The refuge lies within the Big Cypress Swamp physiographic region of Florida. The Swamp covers more than 2,400 square miles of subtropical area in southwest Florida. "Swamp" is a misnomer, for the land contains a variety of wet and dry habitat types. However, the cypress tree is the predominate tree of the area. The Tamiami Limestone formation underlies all of the refuge and is approximately 6 million years old. The formation is capped by hard rock under which are found sand, silts and clays, shell marks, and shell-free, greenish clay. A thin layer of sand, sandy marl, clay and fine shell cover prairie and flatwood areas, while a thicker organic peat ranging in thickness to 7 feet can be found in the hammocks and strands. The refuge is relatively flat, ranging from 11 to 16 feet above mean sea level, with drainage from north to south.

More than 75 percent of the rain normally falls during the six-month wet season of May through October. Summer rains are usually intense, frequent, and short in duration. Winter is a drier period, where rains are usually the result of large frontal systems and are longer in duration, but less intense. Rainfall averages 55 inches per year. During the summer rainy season, shallow depressions fill with water and because of the poor drainage, most of the water remains standing until it evaporates or slowly drains. Thus, as much as 90 percent of the area is inundated to depths ranging from a few inches to more than 3 feet at the height of the rainy season. During the winter drydown, water is concentrated in depressions formed by low spots in the bedrock or the deepest parts of the strands.

The refuge lies within the center of a major watershed that has importance to man and the environment (Figure 13). The Corkscrew Regional Ecosystem Watershed and the Okaloacoochee Slough form the two northern origins of the watershed. Water from these wetlands flows through the refuge and south through the Fakahatchee and Picayune strands into the Ten Thousand Islands coastal area. These wetlands provide flood protection to the urban and agricultural areas of southwest Florida by filling up and holding water from the major rainfall events that frequently occur in south Florida. These wetlands also filter and cleanse these waters before they enter the aquifer and storage reservoirs that are tapped for drinking water. In addition, they provide habitat for a diverse system of plants and animals, unique to Florida and the United States. Most of the remaining Florida panthers, Big Cypress fox squirrels, and

Figure 14. U.S. Fish and Wildlife Refuges within the Big Cypress Watershed

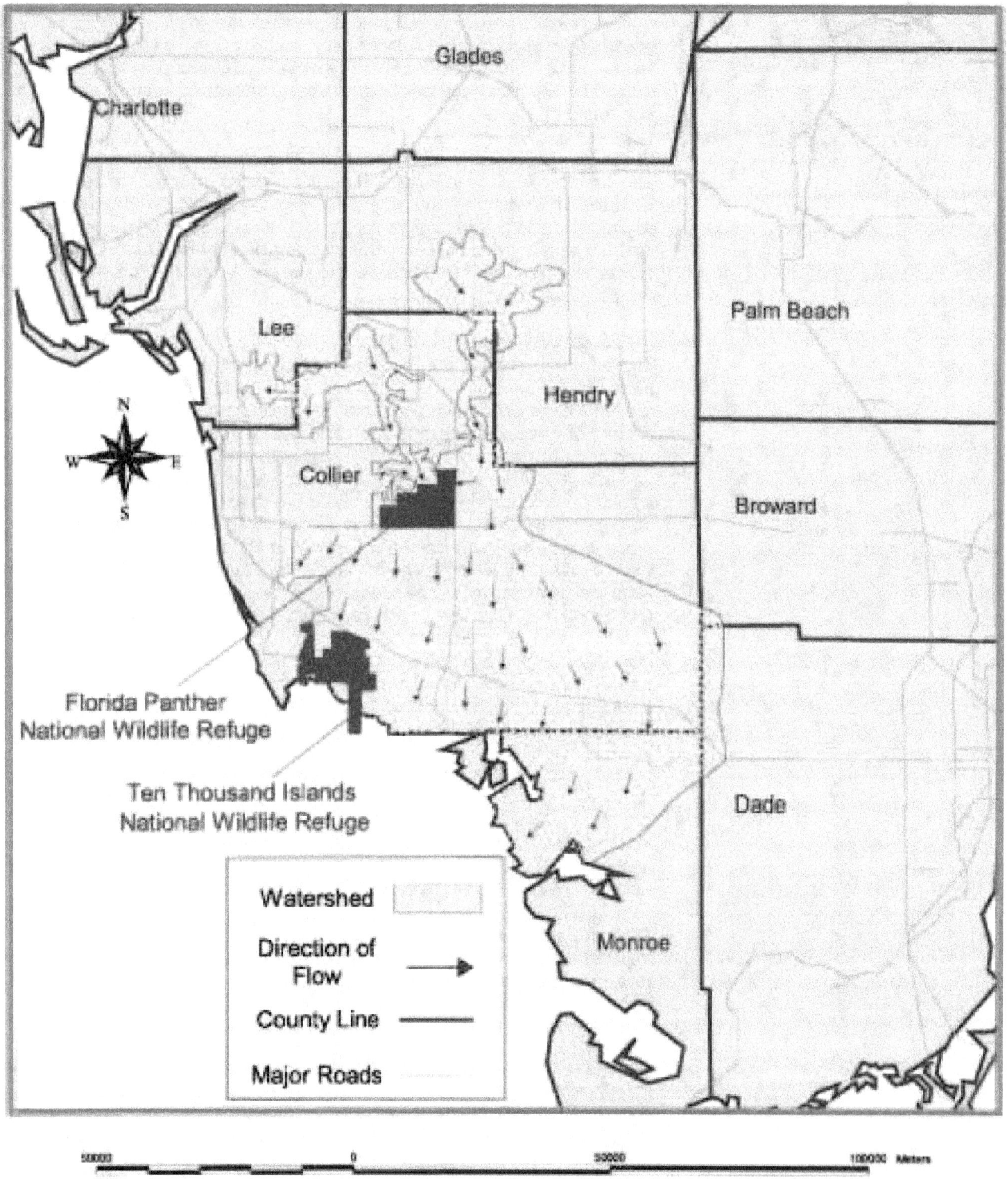

Everglades minks can only be found in this system. Subtropical palms, orchids and other selected tropical plants in this area are found no where else in the United States.

A major agricultural area lies just north of the refuge. Large tracts of lands have been cleared to produce vegetables and citrus. The quantity and quality of the water draining from these operations are undergoing long-term monitoring to determine their impacts on the refuge. Questions persist as to how much of the watershed in private ownership can be developed into agriculture, ranching, or urbanization before major functions and attributes of the wetland ecosystem are lost.

Soils
Soils are predominantly organic peats in the mixed hardwood strand areas ranging in thickness up to 7 feet. A thin layer of mineral soil, especially marl and sand, is dominant on the prairies.

Vegetative Habitats
The Service and others are concerned for the refuge's long-term environmental health and wildlife productivity. Nationwide studies have documented a declining status of numerous vegetative and wetland-dependent wildlife populations. These declines have been attributed to habitat loss and alteration. While the refuge was logged forty to fifty years ago, cypress forests have regrown. However, the adjoining land use has exerted influences to alter refuge habitats. Ditching for residential and agricultural development near the refuge has altered refuge hydrology and has promoted generally drier soils which has promoted an expansion of cabbage palms. More and more it is recognized that the long-term biological health of the refuge is highly dependent upon the ecological health of the watershed.

Wood storks
USFWS photo by Larry W. Richardson

Eight major habitat types have been described for the refuge (Fakahatchee Strand Environmental Assessment 1986). These include:

Mixed Hardwood Swamp Forests:
This community is dominated by diverse hardwoods, including red maple, sweet bay, pop ash, wax myrtle, cocoplum, dahoon holly, myrsine, willow, red bay, and swamp bay. Pure stands of pond apple may grow in the wettest areas, while live oak may dominate on higher ground.

Cypress Forests:
This community type consists of strand, dome, and cypress prairie forests. Pond cypress may dominate, but bald cypress does occur. The strands are common where there is sufficient water and flow to generate a depression channel, but the gradient is low and actual water flow is seldom observed. The strands are elongated, contiguous stands of cypress. Many hardwood species (red bay, swamp bay, wax myrtle, cocoplum) may be interspersed. Domes are characterized by dense, tall pond cypress. Domes occupy depressions in the mineral soil underlain by marl and limestone bedrock. Peat accumulates in the depressions and provides a substrate for the cypress. Similar hardwood species as occur in the strands are also found in the domes. The cypress prairies are also called hatrack or dwarf cypress, because the cypress trees have a stunted growth form and are widely spaced. Rainfall is the most significant source of water for the prairies where vegetation density and diversity are low. Sawgrass, muhly grass, and other herbs and grasses make up the ground vegetation of this prairie.

Prairies:
Prairies are associations of mixed grasses, sedges and other herbaceous plants with few trees. Common species in wet prairie include maidencane, blackhead rush, star dichhromena, muhly, water dropwort, and sawgrass. Common species in dry prairies include saw palmetto, and some of the grasses and sedges found in the pine forest.

Figure 15. Vegetative Habitats Map

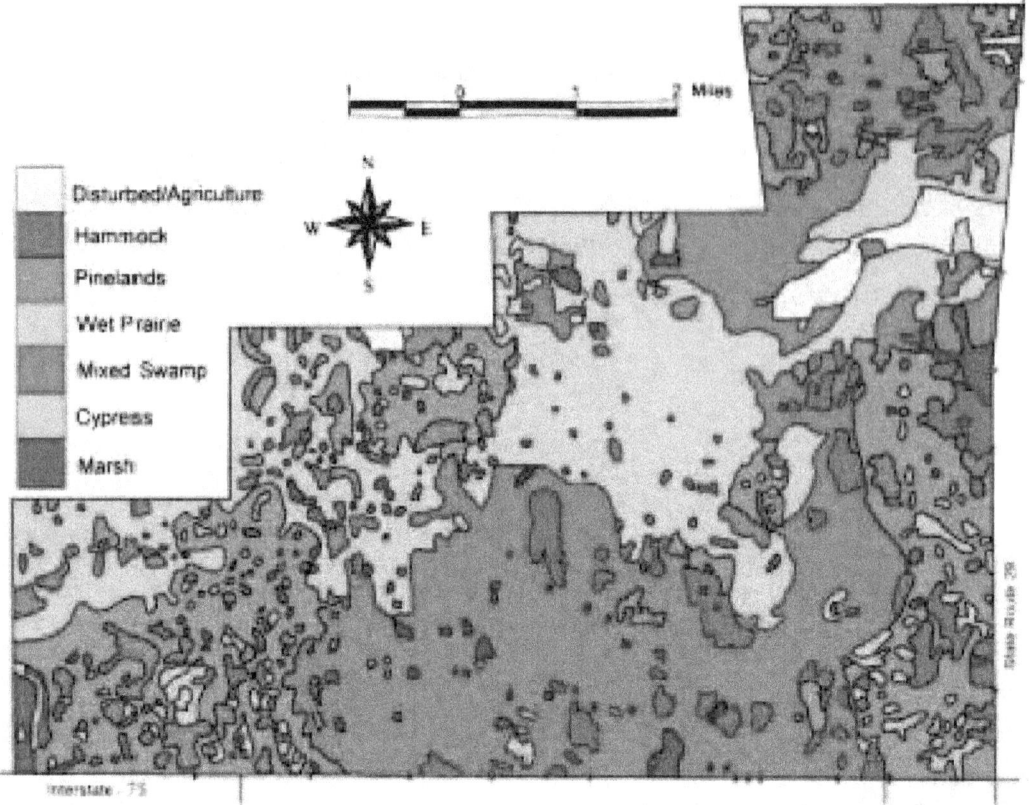

Hammocks:

Hammocks are composed of dense forests of hardwood trees, palms, shrubs, vines, ferns, and numerous epiphytes. They represent climax vegetation on the region and generally possess more tropical species than any of the other community types. Individual hammocks are generally characterized by maple and laurel oak in lower areas, with live oak and cabbage palm on higher areas. Subtropical hammocks support the greatest number of rare and threatened plants. Most of these are epiphytes from the bromeliad, orchid, and fern families.

Mixed Pine and Cypress Forests:

These are open forests of pine, cypress, and cabbage palm. These forests have mixed understory vegetation that ranges from herbaceous plants to hardwood trees.

Pine Forests:

These communities are open forests of southern slash pine, cabbage palm, saw palmetto, and scattered hardwood shrubs and trees.

Pop Ash or Pond Apple Sloughs and Ponds:

These plant communities occur in the deepest drainage area that meanders through the center of the Fakahatchee Strand where, under natural conditions, there would be some water standing year round. The dominate trees are pop ash, pond apple, cypress, willow, and the bays. Plants in the shrub and ground cover zones include buttonbush, leather fern, alligator flag, whitevine and morning glory.

Lakes:

Many small (1-20 acre) lakes are scattered throughout the refuge. The lakes or ponds are shallow (1-4 feet deep), except for Colding and Pistol ponds which have depths of 10-15 feet. These two ponds were artificially excavated for SR 29 road base material. Some common vegetation include pickerel weed, alligator flag, floating lemna and wolffiella, and submergent bladderwort and naiad. A few have emergent stands of giant cutgrass.

Water Resources

The refuge does not have any water control structures or means for water control at this time. However, the Service is involved in a water management project for the west side of the refuge. Lucky Lake Strand and Stumpy Strand are two wetland features comprised of more than 3,000 acres of cypress swamp, mixed swamp, wet prairies, marshes and ponds.

The strands receive water from direct rainfall, and runoff from surrounding uplands and Camp Keais Strand to the north. Natural drainage of these strands changed with the construction of the Golden Gate Estates east of Naples in the 1960s. This project included the excavation of 183 miles of canals to drain wetlands for residential development. South of the refuge, Merritt Canal is one of four canals which drain South Golden Gate Estates into the Faka Union system. In addition to draining large areas along the canal south of I-75, the canal's northern origin is the southern terminus of the Lucky Lake Strand. This resulted in the chronic drainage of both Lucky Lake and Stumpy strands north of the highway.

American alligator
USFWS Photo by Diane Borden-Billiot

The Service has entered into an agreement with the South Florida Water Management District to proceed with the construction of a low-head water control structure on the south side of I-75 at the origin of Merritt Canal. This control structure will be designed to slow the drainage within these two strands to closely match their original hydroperiods. The restoration of this wetland system will enhance the Lucky Lake and Stumpy strands for endangered species, colonial wading birds and waterfowl.

Wildlife Resources

The Florida Panther National Wildlife Refuge is known for its diversity and abundance of wildlife. A total of 126 breeding and non-breeding bird species have been identified; an additional 36 species probably occur on the refuge. Forty-six species of reptiles and amphibians are known to occur on the refuge and another 15 species are known to occur in close proximity to the refuge. Twenty-two species of mammals are known to occur on the refuge and another 11 species are known to occur in close proximity to the refuge. A variety of fish species, representing 13 families, occur in the area.

The Wildlife Inventory Plan, completed in August 1990, is in need of revision to remove ineffective or logistically impractical surveys and inventories and replace them with more accurate and cost effective techniques. Trend data from surveys is still being run and will be evaluated to assist with revisions to the inventory plan that are necessary to help meet the mission of the refuge.

White ibis
USFWS photo by Larry W. Richardson

The following information lists some of the more common species of wildlife found on the refuge:
Neotropical Birds

More than 116 species of neotropical migrants have been recorded in the South Florida Ecosystem. Both resident and migratory passerine birds utilize refuge habitats. The refuge is home to at least 25 species year round with the great crested flycatcher, Carolina wren, northern mockingbird, red bellied woodpecker, and cardinal being the most common species. More than 30 migratory species comprise the majority of passerines that frequent the refuge. Common migrants include tree swallows, American robin, white-eyed vireo, black and white warbler, yellow rumped warbler, palm warbler, and blue-gray gnatcatcher.

The South Florida Ecosystem is located along one of the primary migratory routes for bird species that breed in temperate North America and winter in the tropics of the Caribbean and South America. To further assess the species composition and the abundance of neotropical migrants, the refuge has established a standardized survey across a mostly wooded section of the refuge. This survey is coordinated with the Florida Game and Fresh Water Fish Commission to contribute to the Partners in Flight Program. The survey route is monitored for a minimum of six weeks during the spring and fall migrations. Though this survey route largely traverses woodland habitats, the refuge has enlisted both researchers and volunteers to document as many as 18 other migrant passerines that are thought to occur on the refuge.

Waterfowl

Staff frequently see wood ducks in the ponds, swamps, and flooded buggy trails on the refuge. Due to extensive logging of cypress in the Fakahatchee Strand in the 1940s, there is a lack of nesting cavities. Ducks Unlimited funded a nest box program in 1991 and the station purchased 25 cypress box kits, poles, and other materials. Since their installation in 1991, no wood ducks have used the boxes; however, they have been used by other birds such as screech owls and hooded mergansers.

Marsh and Water Birds

The refuge includes approximately 18,000 acres of wetlands that support a variety of colonial and other wading birds. The most abundant species include wood storks; great blue, little blue, tricolored, and green-backed herons; black and yellow-crowned night-herons; great, snowy, and cattle egrets; white ibis; anhingas; and double-crested cormorants. Approximately six rookeries with 10-50 nests were active this year with a full complement of colonial species, mostly great egrets. Other small rookeries occurred east and southwest of the Hog Pond rookery and in small ponded areas in remote locations on the refuge.

Wood ducks
USFWS Photo

Figure 16. Florida Panther National Wildlife Refuge Wading Bird Roost and Rookery

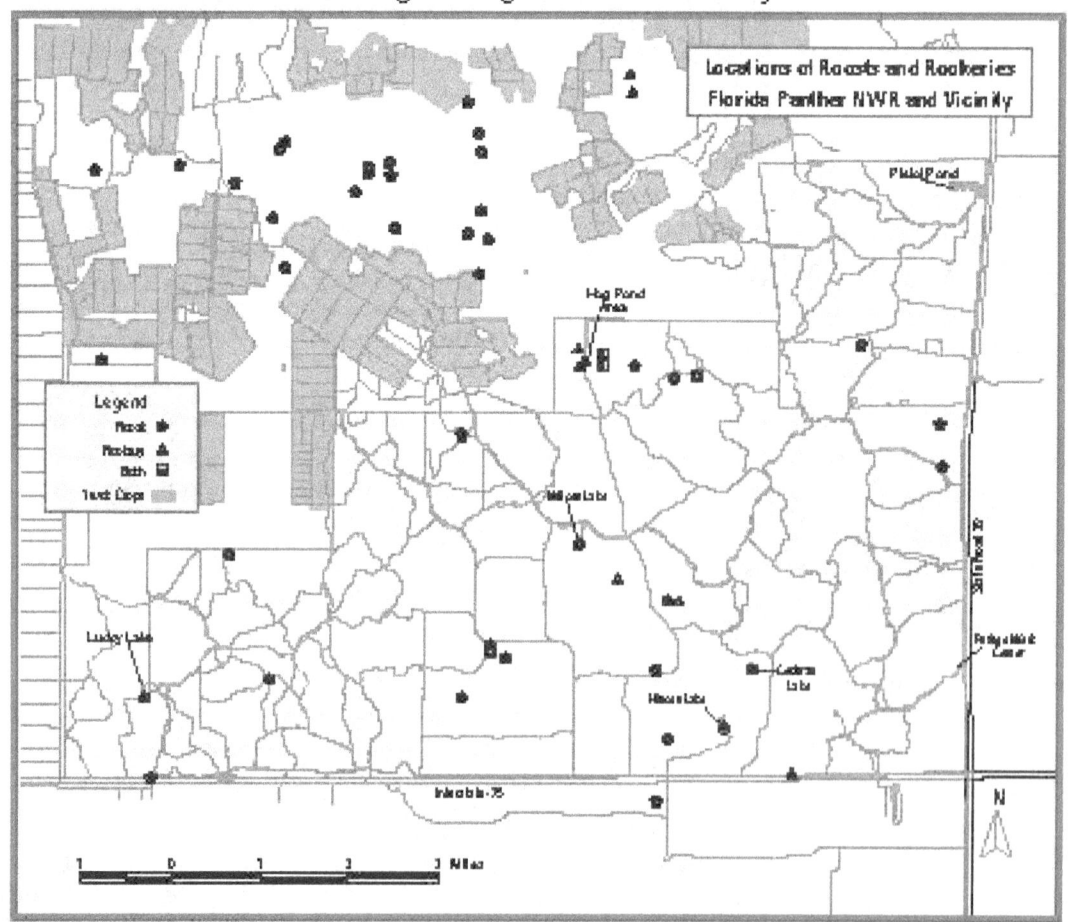

Raptors

Black and turkey vultures are the refuge's most common raptors. Three hundred or more have been observed roosting in trees surrounding a colonial bird roost site on the north end of the refuge. Staff regularly observe red-shouldered and red-tailed hawks, and barred owls are heard. Another noteworthy raptor is the swallow-tailed kite; this species typically utilizes the refuge for nesting as does the red-shouldered hawk. Other raptors that use the refuge during migration, or winter here, include the peregrine falcon, broad-winged hawk, the accipiters, and the northern harrier.

The bald eagle and osprey are residents to the area and are occasionally observed searching for prey over refuge water areas.

Other Resident Birds

The turkey remains a conspicuous game bird on the refuge. Additionally, the Bobwhite quail is found throughout the area but is less conspicuous.

Mammals

Whitetail deer and feral hogs are the most conspicuous game animals on the refuge. Deer and hogs are preferred panther prey species. Hog numbers appear to be stable on the east side of the refuge where they were once hunted by former lessees. Signs of rooting are seen fairly frequently. Groups of and solitary hogs are commonly seen while driving through the eastern side of the refuge. They are infrequently seen at or near the work center off of SR 29.

Raccoons
USFWS photo by Ronald Bell

Raccoons, cottontail rabbits, and nine-banded armadillos are also common. In other areas of South Florida, where deer and hogs are less abundant, these species make up the bulk of the panther's diet. Bobcats and black bears are common on and off the refuge. In the last couple of years, coyotes have begun moving into southwest Florida. So far, tracks on the refuge are infrequently seen. About 33 species of mammals are likely to occur within the refuge; 22 species have been verified by refuge staff.

Fish

The bulk of the aquatic animal biomass in the Fakahatchee Strand is composed of a variety of fish species representing 24 families. The most common species are mosquitofish, flagfish, and least killifish. This fishery is a major link in the food chain in the Fakahatchee Strand.

Population densities fluctuate dramatically from low-density, widely distributed wet season populations to highly concentrated populations found in "gator holes" and other scattered permanent water areas during the dry season. Significant wading bird predation occurs on larger fish during the dry season. The endangered wood stork occasionally utilizes concentrated fish populations as a major food source.

Sport fishing for larger fish species is limited due to the isolation and inaccessibility of fishable waters. Fishing that does occur is directed to accessible canals and road ditches where catfish, sunfish, and largemouth bass can be found. Generally, no significant commercial or subsistence fishing occurs on the project area. At least five species of exotic fish are found on or near the refuge including black acara, oscar, and the mayan cichlid.

Amphibians and Reptiles

Nearly all amphibians depend on aquatic habitats for reproduction and overwintering, and many species are specifically adapted and restricted to the aquatic environments. The greater siren is the largest salamander on the refuge. Other aquatic salamanders common in the area include the two-toed amphiuma and peninsular newt. The most commonly encountered frogs are the green treefrog, Florida cricket frog, and the southern leopard frog.

The American alligator is the largest reptile on the refuge. The black racer, banded water snake, and cottonmouth are probably the most abundant snakes. The most commonly encountered turtle is the peninsula cooter. Although reptiles are generally less dependant on water, a clear preference to aquatic systems is displayed by many turtles, snakes, and alligators. About 61 species of reptiles and amphibians are likely to occur within the refuge; 46 species have been verified by refuge staff.

Endangered and Threatened Species
In addition to the Florida panther, the following additional endangered and threatened species use the refuge. Status designation for each species is shown in parentheses. The Florida grasshopper sparrow, Everglades mink, and red-cockaded woodpecker have not been observed on the refuge.

Mammals
- Florida panther, Felis concolor coryi (E[1], E[2])
- Bobcat, Lynx rufus (CITES II)
- Everglades mink, Mustela vision evergladensis (T[1])
- Florida black bear, Ursus americanus floridanus (T[1])
- Big Cypress fox squirrel, Sciurus niger avicennia (T[1])

Birds
- Southeastern American kestrel, Falco sparverius (T[1], CITES II)
- Wood stork, Mycteria americana (E[1], E[2])
- Snail kite, Rostrhamus sociabilis plumbeus (E[1], E[2])
- Bald eagle, Haliaeetus leucocephalus (T[1], T[2])
- Florida grasshopper sparrow, Ammodramus savannarum (E[1], E[2])
- Little blue heron, Egretta caerulea (SSC)
- Limpkin, Aramus guarauna (SSC)
- Northern harrier, Circus cyaneus (CITES II)
- Red-cockaded woodpecker, Picoides borealis (T[1], E[2])
- Roseate spoonbill, Ajaja ajaja (SSC)
- Florida sandhill crane, Grus canadensis (T[1])
- Snowy egret, Egretta thula (SSC)
- Tricolored heron, Egretta tricolor (SSC)
- White ibis, Eudocimus albus (SSC)

Reptiles
- American alligator, Alligator mississippiensis (SSC, T[2])
- Eastern indigo snake, Drymarchon corias couperi (T[1], T[2])

Federal and State designations of listed species in Florida:
E[1] - State designated endangered species
E[2] - Federally designated endangered species
T[1] - State designated threatened species
T[2] - Federally designated threatened species
SSC - State species of special concern
CITES I and II - Appendix I and II species of the Convention on International Trade in Endangered Species of Wild Fauna and Flora.

The high degree of endemism among south Florida's plants, animals, and biotic communities – combined with extensive land conversion and habitat degradation by humans – has imperiled many of the region's species. The South Florida Ecosystem supports 70 federally threatened or endangered species. Eight of these species are known to utilize the refuge.

Cultural Resources
Archaeological investigations within the refuge have been limited. Seventeen archaeological and historic sites are recorded for the refuge. Two additional prehistoric sites have been reported but have not been verified. The three prehistoric sites are black earth middens and date to an unspecified Glades period. The middens contain a variety of ceramics, worked bone and shell tools, and faunal materials. Similar sites are seen in the Big Cypress National Preserve. Eleven of the historic sites are 20th century hunting camps. Buildings stand only at the Wilson Lake and Rock

American alligator
USFWS Photo by Diane Border-Elliot

Island camps. The Lee Tidewater Cypress Company purchased the Fakahatchee Strand in 1906 for its large virgin stands of cypress. Logging operations did not begin until the late 1940s. Miccosukee and Seminole bands may have utilized the refuge in the 19th and early 20th centuries. However, no sites or camps have been found or reported on the refuge which can be attributed to either group.

Today, the only visible evidence are the all terrain vehicle roads which crisscross the refuge. The roads were the railbeds of the lumber railroad. A shell rock mining and crushing company operated near Pistol Pond as evidenced by the scatter of rusting equipment. The Colding House, located at the refuge maintenance complex, originally stood near the fire tower. It was moved to its current location in 1950. None of the historic sites are considered eligible for the National Register of Historic Places.

Socioeconomic Environment

Collier County was established in 1923 by the Florida State Legislature from a portion of Lee and Monroe counties. It is located on the southern Gulf coast of the Florida peninsula due west of the Miami-Ft. Lauderdale area. Naples, located in the western coastal area of Collier County, is the largest incorporated city and serves as the county seat. Everglades City, the only other incorporated city within the county, lies south and east of Naples.

Modern-day settlement of the county evolved in isolated pockets during the 1870s while the region was still a part of Monroe County. In 1887, it became part of Lee County and remained such for 36 years until July 7, 1923, when Collier County was established.

Settlement began in the county in the mid 1870s, and in 1995 the county's population was 186,504. According to the Growth Management Plan, Collier County contains approximately 2,025.45 square miles of land area, and is one of the largest counties east of the Mississippi River. It is larger than the State of Rhode Island and also the State of Delaware.

Of all the Florida counties, Collier is the least known. With the exception of Naples and Immokalee, the communities are widely scattered in sparsely populated pockets along the coast and interior. Only the extensive development of Marco Island and North Naples in recent years has altered the established pattern of growth, which has evolved in the rural and island settlements over the last century and a half.

However, this rural lifestyle is destined to change in the coming years, as the region experiences astounding urban growth, and more communities expand and others develop to meet the needs of an increased residential and (tourist) population. While there were only 16,000 people living in the county in 1960, the population is expected to increase to nearly 350,000 by the year 2020 (Enterprise Florida, Inc.), with a current annual growth rate of 68.60 percent (compared to a state growth rate of only 27.95 percent). Collectively, the entire southwest Florida region is, and will continue to be, one of the fastest growing regions in the United States.

For business owners and employees alike, Collier County offers an opportunity without comparison. For residents and tourists, the as yet unspoiled southwest Florida coast offers a myriad of living and recreational opportunities. Unfortunately, the very growth and development which makes southwest Florida such an alluring place for so many also threatens the natural habitat mosaic of the region. Special, coordinated efforts from all stakeholders involved with south Florida issues will be necessary to not only preserve the quality of the national environment in the region, but the quality of life for southwest Florida's residents and visitors as well.

Refuge Management Programs
Prescribed Burning
Prescribed burning is the primary refuge management tool used to maintain native plant communities. Historically, this area was burned by wildfires ignited by lightning or infrequent prescribed burns set by Native Americans and later individuals who sought to improve habitat conditions for hunting and for cattle. Prescribed fire is a well established and effective habitat management tool. Proper use of prescribed fire in appropriate plant communities will maintain existing subclimax successional stages and maximize overall productivity. The burns also produce an abundance of green browse and other improved forage conditions that greatly benefit whitetail deer, the primary prey species of the panther. Also, the use of prescribed fire significantly reduces the size and intensity of wildfires in the area.

Due to the limited burning of the refuge prior to establishment, fuel loads were initially quite heavy. Fuel loads of 100- to 300-tons-per-acre in the pine/palmetto habitat complex were common. These types of loads produce hot, dangerous, and difficult fires to control. Initial refuge burns were conducted during the winter months, when temperatures, relative humidity, and water levels facilitated the prescriptions. Warm season prescribed burns are being implemented and evaluated as to their benefits.

Controlled burn
Photo by Elise Smith

Figure 17. Refuge facilities and Prescribed Fire Compartments with Rotation-Year

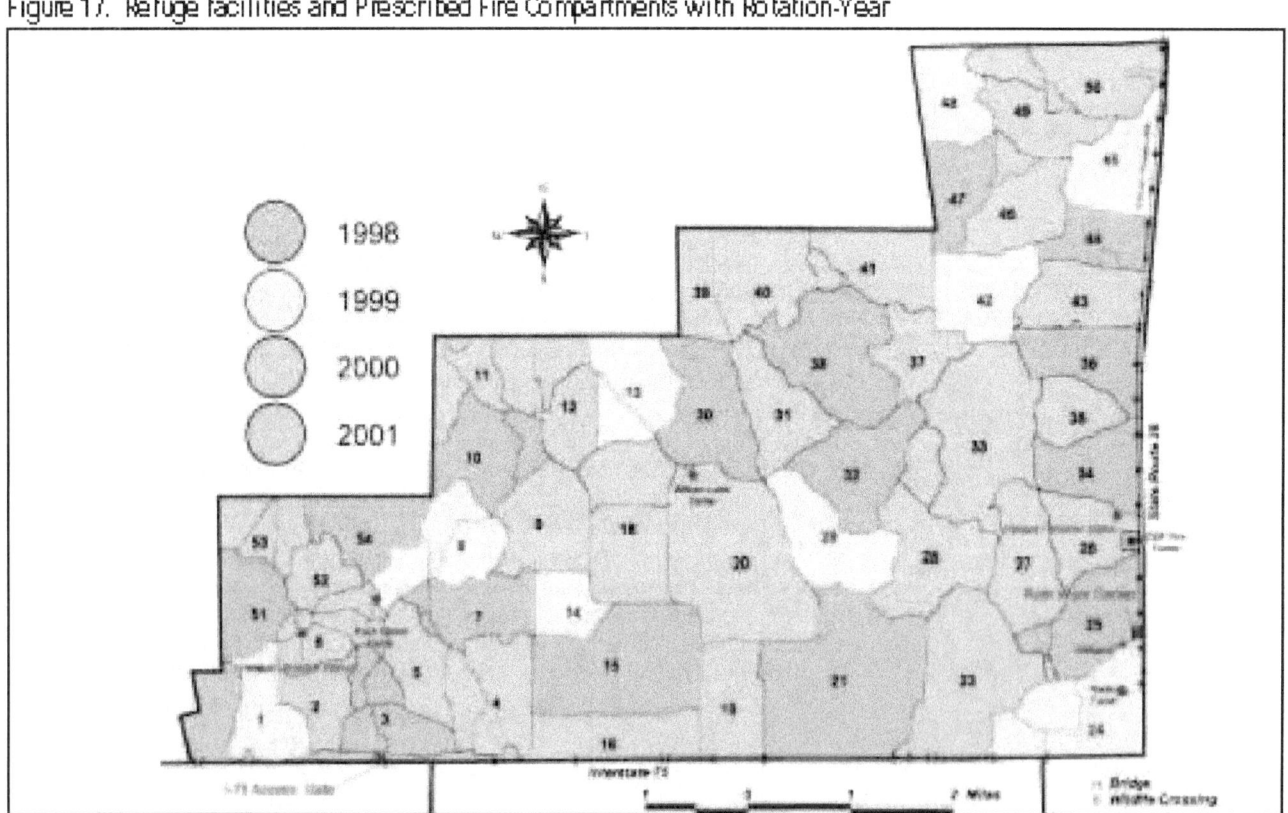

Whitetail deer
Photo by Fred Youngblood

Deer Forage Enhancement

Another management technique is food plots for deer forage enhancement. The refuge whitetail deer population is estimated to be approximately 9 deer per-square-mile. This number is lower than other habitats north of the refuge and other parts of the southeast. We believe this condition is a reflection of the refuge's poor forage quality due to impoverished nutritional conditions of the soil.

The refuge is researching several methods of supplemental feeding of deer and other wildlife. There are three primary objectives to the research: (1) production/provision of supplemental forage and grain to augment native diets and thereby enhance wildlife populations; (2) research and documentation of farming practices that benefit wildlife; and (3) improvement of soils through incorporation of organic matter and nitrogen. Planting food plots and distributing grain (shelled corn) through automated feeders are the primary methods of implementing the study. Through these methods the refuge will determine the benefits of supplemental feeding and share this information with other land managers wanting to improve panther prey numbers.

Exotic Plant Control

Invasive exotic plants are controlled to protect native habitats. The refuge is fortunate to not have established melaleuca populations. However, each year a few new trees are found and immediately cut down and treated with herbicides.

Brazilian pepper, on the other hand, is well established on the refuge. Control rather than eradication is the realistic goal for dealing with this aggressive alien invader. Cogon grass, old world climbing fern, and torpedo grass have also been treated with herbicides.

Public Use

Because of specific efforts to optimize conditions for the panther, the refuge has remained closed to general public access and use. Occasional swamp buggy tours are given to small groups. Additionally, refuge staff participate in environmental education programs at local schools and public events.

Environmental Consequences

The following discussion assesses the environmental impacts associated with the approval and implementation of a comprehensive conservation plan for the refuge. Each alternative is discussed separately. The issues identified in the Affected Environment section above, as well as some of the issues identified in the planning process for the plan are considered below.

Alternative A: No Action

Climate:
This alternative would have no impact on the climate.

Air Quality:
Basically, this alternative would have no impact on air quality. Some short-term impacts would continue to occur due to the continued implementation of prescribed burning that this alternative advocates. Burning is required for habitat improvement to reduce the invasion of exotic plants and dense woody vegetation and maintain those plant communities that are fire dependent. Although burning would cause a temporary degradation of local air quality, the area is sparsely populated and therefore would have little effect on human environment. No long-term or adverse effects to air quality would occur.

Water Resources:
Under the No Action Alternative, the quantity and quality of the water could be negatively impacted over the long run. Currently, the refuge has no water management guidelines to aid in setting management objectives.

The Service has entered into an agreement with the South Florida Water Management District to proceed with the construction of a low-head water control structure on the south side of I-75 at the origin

Roseate spoonbill
USFWS Photo

of Merritt Canal. This control structure will slow the drainage within these two strands closely matching their original hydroperiods. The restoration of this wetland system will enhance the Lucky Lake and Stumpy strands for endangered species, colonial wading birds, and waterfowl.

Other than the current agreement with the water district, this alternative would not provide any direction for the refuge to actively develop partnerships and cooperative agreements with other jurisdictions and private landowners to protect the water resources in the Big Cypress Watershed. Additionally, no measures to protect the watershed from development activities would be pursued, therefore, agricultural and residential development around the refuge would continue to be a threat that could seriously impact water quality.

Soils:

The soils of the refuge could be subjected to accelerated soil loss under this alternative. The loss of water to drainage, redirection, or agricultural use will tend to dry out the soils of the refuge and facilitate soil loss to oxidation and erosion. The causes for drier soil is due to current ditching practices being completed for residential and agricultural areas adjacent to the refuge. These ditching practices have altered natural water flow through the refuge thus promoting drier soils and expansion of cabbage palms.

Vegetative Habitats and Habitat Management:

Under the No Action Alternative, habitat management would remain focused on the refuge for the Florida panther. Additionally, prescribed burning would continue to be the primary habitat management tool. Proper use of this tool and the extent to its effectiveness would not be totally understood due to lack of research and data analysis. Presently, the refuge fire program is sufficient enough to provide adequate green browse for whitetail deer which is the primary prey species for the panther.

This alternative would continue to provide important habitat for various songbirds and other wildlife but at levels considerably below their potential. Encroachment of invasive exotic vegetation would continue to the detriment of native cypress swamp lands, and give way to increased levels of undesirable vegetation.

Wildlife Diversity:

Panthers would remain the primary focus and, presumably, would continue to use the refuge in high numbers due to active management practices. Due to the loss of historical habitat conditions on the landscape, biological diversity would not be appropriately managed under this alternative. Native cypress swamp would continue to be lost to encroaching invasive exotic plants and woody vegetation.

Missed opportunities to improve habitat, wildlife, and overall biological diversity on non-refuge lands would result because there would be no strategies developed to coordinate with other jurisdictions and private landowners.

Endangered and Threatened Species:

Certain species of concern would benefit under this alternative, namely, the panther. As noted, most management projects would revolve around the protection and enhancement of the panther and its habitat.

Because management would primarily focus on the panther, it would result in missed opportunity to achieve cumulative enhancement of biological diversity and threatened and endangered species management. Populations of the remaining species of concern, including the wood stork, snail-kite, bald eagle, Florida grasshopper sparrow, red-cockaded woodpecker, and eastern indigo snake, would probably remain at current levels because management would focus more on the panther.

Again, there would be no strategies developed to work cooperatively with landowners in the surrounding areas to effect sustainable resource management. Management practices on private lands have a significant effect to the overall health of the watershed. If unsound land and water use practices were employed, threatened and endangered species on the refuge would be impacted.

Public Use, Compatibility, and Environmental Education:

Under the No Action Alternative, the public use and environmental education programs would continue to be operated in their current state. Public use would not be allowed and would conflict with the goals of this plan of action. This alternative would result in limited environmental and public education opportunities. Educational programs would be given upon request, but no formal outreach would be employed. The office headquarters would continue to serve as the visitor contact station; however, no efforts would be made to install educational materials or displays at the refuge and thousands of people traveling I-75 would miss an opportunity to learn about the panther, refuge, and refuge system. Another missed opportunity to work in conjunction with interest groups on an interpretive trail would also result.

Cultural Resources:
Under this alternative, the current program does not provide for the implementation of specific cultural resource protection strategies. Lack of clear direction on how to handle cultural resource issues could have a negative impact to the cultural resources sites on the refuge.

Socioeconomic Aspects:
This alternative would not provide for increased revenues to the local economy because public use would remain at minimal levels. The refuge would be unable to improve the local environmental and refuge awareness substantially due to the small public outreach program. Public goals for endangered panther preservation and enhancement would not be achieved.

Alternative B: Ecosystem Approach (Proposed and Preferred Alternative)
Climate:
This alternative would have no effect on the climate.

Air Quality:
Some short-term impacts are likely to occur due to the continued implementation of prescribed burning that this alternative advocates. Burning is required for habitat improvement to reduce the invasion of exotic plants and dense woody vegetation and allow for maintaining a mosaic pattern of native landscapes. Although burning would cause a temporary degradation of local air quality, the area is sparsely populated and, therefore, would have little effect on human environment. No long-term or adverse effects to air quality would occur.

Water Resources:
The water quantity and quality under the Preferred Alternative would be further protected. Strategies would be developed that would ensure sound use of the surface and ground water. It is anticipated that the water quality would remain the same or would improve under this alternative. In creating partnerships and working cooperatively with private landowners in the Big Cypress Swamp watershed and the United States, strategies would be employed that would minimize existing impacts of land and water use practices that currently affect water resources.

Computer modeling in cooperation with the South Florida Water Management District will aid significantly in developing water management guidelines for the refuge and calls for regular monitoring of baseline information (pH, total dissolved oxygen, contaminants). Ultimately, the model will be able to predict the impacts that development will have on the surface and ground water, so that a plan of action can be strategically developed to protect the valuable water supply.

Blue-winged teal
USFWS Photo by Ted Hover

Soils:
The management activities described in the Ecosystem Approach will have minimal effects on the geology and soils of the refuge. Any mechanical control methods used to remove or open up dense stands of woody, invader vegetation could negatively impact refuge soils. However, restoring these areas to their native vegetative state would ultimately result in reduced soil loss. Because fire historically played an important role in maintaining native vegetation, any implemented prescribed burns should have minimal effects on refuge soils. To prevent soil loss and erosion after burning, slope factors will be carefully considered.

There are no proposed developments such as trails, roads, or buildings on the refuge that would affect refuge soils. Recreational uses such as hiking are expected to be minimal and will not result in significant, if any, impacts to the soils. Existing refuge roads would continue to be maintained with little or no impacts.

Vegetative Habitats and Habitat Management:
Habitat management is planned and desirable and would result in more natural, diverse habitats which in turn would effect overall increased biological diversity on the refuge. Habitat management practices would be employed that would restore various habitats (particularly green browse and other forage conditions) that greatly benefit whitetail deer, the primary prey species of the panther. Encouraging native vegetation would provide an increased forage and cover base for native wildlife and would also increase infiltration rates and reduce runoff and evaprotranspiration rates. All of this would help maintain water flows that fish and other wildlife depend on for their survival.

Under this alternative, orchids and other plants, as well as large expanses of cypress and mixed grass prairies and aquatic habitats, would continue to be managed and protected with beneficial results. As mentioned previously, water management strategies would be developed as a result of the computer model. Additionally, partnerships with private landowners and other agencies such as the South Florida Water Management District that effect sound use of the watershed would be implemented. Construction of low-head water control structures would slow drainage of wetland areas. Routine maintenance work such as removing non-native species would ensure continued water flows.

Wildlife Diversity:
The Ecosystem Approach is designed to enhance fish and wildlife populations, resulting in overall increased diversity. This approach would provide an opportunity for maximizing land and habitat protection for the benefit of native wildlife populations. Strategies would be developed in conjunction with landowners (public and private) to preserve a mosaic pattern of native landscapes that would support diverse, flourishing communities of plant and animal species. It also calls for management practices that would optimize historical habitat characteristics to improve wildlife diversity. Water development and enhancement, vegetation thinning, prescribed burning, and restoration of native cypress and mixed-grass prairies would all further enhance species richness.

Endangered and Threatened Species:
Threatened, endangered, and species of concern would benefit in this alternative. Currently, there are 21 species of mammals, birds, and reptiles found in the vicinity of the refuge that fit into this category. Active management practices would be centered around the recovery and enhancement of these species, with major emphasis on the panther.

Management strategies to aid in panther recovery would include cooperating with other agencies and landowners, managing existing habitats and populations, determining biological requirements of the panther, protecting historic habitat, assessing habitats for reintroduction into historic ranges, controlling invasive exotic plants, and developing information and education programs for the panther.

Along with the management framework strategies for the panther, management strategies for the other federally listed species would be incorporated to provide improved nesting habitat and vegetation manipulation for the wood stork, construction of nesting structures for the bald eagle, investigation of varied prescribed burning patterns for the Florida grasshopper sparrow and other passerines, transplantation and habitat improvement for the red-cockaded woodpecker, and continued releases of confiscated eastern indigo snakes. Although the snail kite is an occasional visitor to the refuge, no plans have been made to directly improve its habitat. However, the snail kite will benefit from other plan management strategies.

Public Use, Compatibility, and Environmental Education:

The refuge was established to provide habitat for the endangered Florida panther. Secondary access, such as hunting, fishing, and interpretive and recreational trails on the refuge would depend greatly on their impact upon the panther and other resources.

If hunting were permitted, it would include whitetail deer, turkey, and hog species. These activities would would be coordinated with the Florida Game and Fresh Water Fish Commission and would have to be based upon population survey data. Seasonality of the activity will be a component of the compatibility analysis as well as Section 7 consultation based biological evaluations. Additionally, should these activities be determined compatible and not in conflict with the Endangered Species Act, and should the Service decide to implement them, additional National Environmental Policy Act analysis may be necessary.

In addition, increased use of the refuge may conflict with existing and planned research and management programs. These programs would take precedence over secondary use activities because the programs directly support the purpose of the refuge.

Currently, there is no public access to the refuge. Activities such as hunting, fishing, and interpretive and recreational trails on the refuge would depend greatly on their potential impacts to the panther, other resources, and refuge programs. A decision to allow or disallow those types of uses should be based on the results of research and management activities that are presently occurring on the refuge or being proposed for the refuge.

The development of a short interpretive trail and waterbird viewing area, placed in areas of least use by panthers, would not adversely affect the animal and would greatly promote awareness of refuge programs and the plight of the panther and other refuge resources. This form of access would be allowed and developed immediately.

The Service, in partnership with other agencies, is seeking to offer a multi-agency visitor center and environmental center on the SR 29 and I-75 interchange. Strategies have been developed in the plan to pursue the installation of a visitor center and environmental education classroom.

Opportunities for environmental education would be promoted in an "off refuge" approach due to the sensitive nature of threatened and endangered species on the refuge. Outreach to children and other segments of the population would be developed by designing environmental programs tailored to fit the needs of local schools from elementary to high school levels, and by giving presentations at local community events and to various interest groups.

Cultural Resources:

Implementation of the Ecosystem Approach would result in compliance with all Service and other applicable federal laws to provide the fullest protection possible to the cultural resources on the refuge. It would ensure that all appropriate measures are taken to protect the resources prior to any undertakings that could potentially impact them. Visitor use and associated effects would be monitored through appropriate law enforcement efforts. Any new cultural resource sites and objects found on the refuge would be reported immediately to the Regional Historic Preservation Officer in order to ensure investigation in a timely manner.

Socioeconomic Aspects:

The adoption of the Ecosystem Approach alternative is not anticipated to have significant negative effects to the socioeconomics in the area. The Service expects an overall benefit to the local economy based on implementation of this alternative. It establishes added flexibility with respect to the overall compatible uses of the area. These features would probably result in visitors choosing to stay longer in the Naples area thereby benefitting local merchants and commerce in general.

Additionally, the Service proposes to investigate the feasibility of expanding refuge hours and the development of cooperative ventures with the local Chamber of Commerce. All of these proposed changes to the refuge program would encourage increases in tourism in a structured and strategic manner. The controlled access system would allow the refuge to effectively monitor increases and then make management adjustments based on visitation levels. The refuge program, in combination with the public visitation program at the Big Cypress National Preserve, and other state managed areas, provides strong support to the economics of the local community.

Alternative C: Maximum Habitat Developments and Public Use Programs

Climate:

This alternative would have no impact on the climate.

Air Quality:

This alternative would temporarily impact the air quality as a result of implementation of intense prescribed burns to restore native vegetation habitats. No long-term impacts would occur.

Water Resources:

Under this alternative, the quantity and quality of the water could be negatively impacted over the long run. No water management guidelines to aid in setting management objectives would be pursued.

Other than the current agreement with the water district, this alternative would not provide any direction for the refuge to actively develop partnerships and cooperative agreements with other jurisdictions and private landowners to protect the water resources in the Big Cypress Watershed. Additionally, no measures to protect the watershed from development activities would be pursued, therefore, agricultural and residential development around the refuge would continue to be a threat that could seriously impact water quality.

Soils:

This alternative would call for more developed facilities to accommodate increased public use on the refuge. The construction of facilities such as a visitor station, trails, parking areas, and restrooms would have significant impacts to the soil on the refuge. Soils would be disturbed by the construction of dikes, roads, parking areas, and other visitor facilities. Drainage, hydroperiod, and sheetwater flow may also be adversely impacted by visitor access routes. This may cause soils to dry out or become waterlogged depending upon the circumstance.

Vegetative Habitats and Habitat Management:

Under this alternative, intensive habitat management practices would be widely employed to restore historic native vegetation. Wetland habitats would be extensively developed and recreated to maximize the water resources for the benefit of native wildlife. Panther habitat and native ecosystem restoration on the refuge would be maximized. This would be achieved through thinning and opening of the dense vegetative areas, prescribed burning, and aggressive exotic plant control.

Wildlife Diversity:

Wildlife using the refuge would benefit from the enhanced management and research programs. The refuge would experience increased diversity of avifauna such as waterfowl, shorebirds, and other waterbirds. With restoration of historic vegetation, overall biological diversity would increase and biological values would considerably increase. However, these increases may or may not positively impact the panther.

Wildlife diversity would be expected to decline in areas off the refuge without programs to cooperatively manage and protect watershed resources.

Endangered and Threatened Species:

This alternative's habitat management practices should have beneficial impacts to threatened and endangered species on the refuge. Most of these species, including the panther, wood stork, snail kite, bald eagle, Florida grasshopper sparrow, red-cockaded woodpecker, and eastern indigo snake, that rely on the wetlands for their survival, would expand their populations due to increased available refuge habitats.

Increased public use may have a detrimental effect on panthers; subsequent studies would document the impacts. In addition panthers and other endangered species would be expected to decline in areas off the refuge without programs to cooperatively manage and protect watershed resources.

Public Use, Compatibility, and Environmental Education:

The main impact from this alternative would be from intense development of facilities to accommodate increased visitation by the public. This would require a significant increase in base funding and staff in order to effectively manage the program. Building of the facilities would result in disturbances and losses of some habitat types. Expansion of the number and kind of users permitted could create conflicts between user groups such as hunters and wildlife observers.

The environmental education program would be actively promoted and developed on the refuge. Self-guided trails and auto loops would be developed with appropriate interpretive material displayed along the way. Tours of the refuge would be given to groups interested in the management of native habitats and their associated fish and wildlife species.

Increases in the public use and environmental education programs could negatively impact refuge resources. The refuge would be susceptible to trampling of aquatic, riparian, and other habitats due to increased foot traffic, as well as littering and disturbances to native wildlife. Another threat is the possibility of exotic fish introductions which have occurred in the past.

Cultural Resources:

This alternative would provide for greater public interpretation of historic and archaeological resources on the refuge. Refuge interpretation would mostly be in conjunction with the exhibits associated with historic uses, however, other cultural resource sites associated with the refuge would be opened up for interpretation as well. This would require the development of roads, trails, exhibits, and displays. Increased visitation to the sites could increase vandalism, pot hunting, and casual taking of artifacts. Law enforcement activities would need to be stepped up considerably in order to prevent such violations.

Socioeconomic Aspects:
This alternative would have significant impacts on socioeconomic aspects related to the local community. Increased visitation to the refuge would bring increased revenues to the local contractors for construction of the extensive aquatic/wetland developments and the public use and educational facilities. With the enhancement of environmental education programs, the refuge would be able to meet its public outreach goals and objectives.

Figure 18. Summary of Environmental Consequences by Alternative

Environmental Impact Areas	Alternative A No Action Alternative	Alternative B (Proposed) Ecosystem Approach	Alternative C Maximum Habitat Development and Public Use Programs
Climate			
Air Quality			
Water Resources	x	xx	
Soils	x		
Vegetative Habitats and Habitat Management	x	xx	xx
Wildlife Diversity	x	xx	x
Endangered and Threatened Species	x	xx	x
Public Use, Compatibility, and Environmental Education		xx	x
Cultural Resources		xx	x
Socioeconomic Aspects		xx	x

x - minimal positive effects
xx - maximum positive effects

Cumulative Impacts

All of the above alternatives were evaluated as to their cumulative impacts. Cumulative impacts include impacts on the environment which result from incremental effects of the proposed action when added to other past, present, and reasonably foreseeable future actions. Cumulative impacts can result from individually minor, but collectively significant, actions taking place over a period of time.

Implementing Alternative B would reduce any potential for cumulative impacts because of the strategic approach to managing refuge programs including wildlife-dependent public uses, and the consideration of resource conflicts and opportunities within a broad management framework. This would be a change from the issue-by-issue, problem-by-problem fragmented approach inherent to the No Action Alternative.

Where site development activities are to be proposed during the next 5 to 10 years, each activity would be given the appropriate NEPA consideration. At that time, any required mitigation activities, if necessary, would be designed in the specific project to reduce the level of impacts to the human environment and to protect fish and wildlife and their habitats.

Mitigation and Residual Impacts of the Proposed/Preferred Action

No mitigation would be necessary in the adoption and implementation of the proposed/preferred action. Where site development activities will be proposed during the next 15 years, each activity would be given the appropriate NEPA consideration. At that time, any required mitigation activities would be designed into the specific project to reduce any significant adverse impacts to the environment. Long-term monitoring will help in determining actual effects and how the Service should respond.

- The refuge would closely regulate any proposed activities to lessen any potential impacts such as restricting use to seasons when known breeding and nesting activities are at a minimum.

- The refuge would prohibit any activities in areas where endangered species would be negatively affected.

- The refuge would monitor uses and establish a system to keep track of numbers of users and adjust activity levels accordingly.

Photo by D. W. Pfitzer

Legal Mandates

This section outlines current legal, policy, and administrative guidelines for the management of national wildlife refuges. It begins with the more general considerations such as laws and Executive Orders of the Service, and moves toward those guidelines that apply specifically to the Florida Panther National Wildlife Refuge.

This unit also includes sections dealing with specially designated sites such as historical landmarks and archaeological sites, all of which carry with them specific direction by law and/or policy. In addition, consideration is given to guidance prompted by other formal and informal natural resource planning and research efforts.

All the legal, policy, and administrative planning guidelines provide the framework within which management activities are proposed and developed. This guidance also provides the framework for the enhancement of cooperation between the refuge and other surrounding jurisdictions in the ecosystem.

Administration of the refuges takes into account a myriad of bills passed by the United States Congress and signed into law by the President of the United States. These statutes are considered to be the law of the land as areExecutive Orders promulgated by the President. The following is a list of most of the pertinent statutes establishing legal parameters and policy direction to the National Wildlife Refuge System. Included are those statutes and mandates pertaining to the management of the refuge.

For those laws that provide special guidance and have strong implications relevant to the Service or the refuge, legal summaries are offered below. Many of the summaries have been taken from **The Evolution of National Wildlife Law** by Michael J. Bean.[1] For the bulk of applicable laws and other mandates, legal summaries are available upon request.

Summary of Congressional Acts, Treaties, and other Legal Acts that Relate to Administration of the National Wildlife Refuge System:

1.   Lacey Act of 1900, as amended (16 U.S.C. 701).

2.   Antiquities Act of 1906 (16 U.S.C. 431).

3.   Migratory Bird Treaty Act of 1918 (16 U.S.C. 703-711) and 1978 (40 Stat. 755).

4.   Migratory Bird Conservation Act, (1929) as amended. (16 U.S.C. 715-715s).

5.   Migratory Bird Hunting Stamp Act of 1934, (U.S.C. 718-718h).

6.   Fish and Wildlife Coordination Act, (1934) as amended (16 U.S.C. 661-666).

   The Act is "the first major federal wildlife statute to employ the strategy of compelling consideration of wildlife impacts. The act authorized 'investigations to determine the effects of domestic sewage, trade wastes, and other polluting substances on wildlife, encouraged the development of a program for the maintenance of an adequate supply of wildlife on the public domain' and other federally owned lands, and called for state and federal cooperation in developing a nationwide program of wildlife conservation and rehabilitation."[2]

---

[1] Bean, Michael J., 1983. **The Evolution of National Wildlife Law**, Praeger Publishers, New York.
[2] Ibid., pp. 181.

7. Historic Sites Act of 1935 (16 U.S.C. 461).

The Act declared it a national policy to preserve historic sites and objects of national significance, including those located on refuges. It provided procedures for designation, acquisition, administration, and protection of such sites. National Historic and Natural Landmarks are designated under authority of this Act. As of January 1989, 31 national wildlife refuges contained such sites.

8. Convention Between the United States of America and the Mexican States for the Protection of Migratory Birds and Game Mammals, (1936) (50 Sta. 1311).

9. Convention of Nature Protection and Wildlife Preservation in the Western Hemisphere, 1940 (56 Stat. 1354).

10. Fish and Wildlife Act of 1956, as amended (16 U.S.C. 742-742j).

11. Refuge Recreation Act, as amended, (Public Law 87-714.76 Sta. 653; 16 U.S.C. 460k-4) September 28, 1962.

This Act authorizes the Secretary of the Interior "to administer areas of the System 'for public recreation when in his/her judgement public recreation can be an appropriate incidental or secondary use; provided, that such public recreation use shall be permitted only to the extent that it is practicable and not inconsistent with the primary objectives for which each particular area is established.' Recreational uses 'not directly related to the primary purposes and functions of the individual areas' of the System may also be permitted, but only upon an determination by the Secretary that they 'will not interfere with the primary purposes' of the refuges and that funds are available for their development, operation, and maintenance."[3]

12. Refuge Revenue Sharing Act of 1964, (16 U.S.C. 715s) as amended (P.L. 95-469, approved 10-17-78).

The Act provides "that the net receipt from the 'sale or other disposition of animals, timber, hay, grass, or other products of the soil, minerals, shells, sand, or gravel, from other privileges, or from leases for public accommodations or facilities in connection with the operation and management of areas of the National Wildlife Refuge System shall be paid into a special fund. The monies from the fund are then to be used to make payments for public schools and roads to the counties in which refuges having such revenue producing activities are located."[4]

13. Land and Water Conservation Fund Act of 1965, as amended (16 U.S.C. 460L-4 to 460L-11), and as amended through 1987.

14. National Wildlife Refuge System Administration Act of 1966 (16 U.S.C. 668dd-668ee).

This Act, derived from sections 4 and 5 of Public Law 89-669, "consolidated 'game ranges,' 'wildlife ranges,' 'wildlife management areas,' 'waterfowl production areas,' and 'wildlife refuges,' into a single 'National Wildlife Refuge System.' It (1) placed restrictions on the transfer, exchange, or other disposal of lands within the system; (2) clarified the Secretary's authority to accept donations of money to be used for land acquisition; and (3) most importantly, authorized the Secretary, under regulations, to 'permit the use of any area within the System for any purpose, including but not limited to hunting, fishing, public recreation and accommodations, and access whenever he determines that such uses are compatible with the major purposes for which such areas were established.'"[5]

[3] Ibid., pp. 125-126.
[4] Ibid., pp. 126.
[5] Ibid., pp. 125.

15. National Historic Preservation Act of 1966 (16 U.S.C. 470).

Public Law 89-665 as repeatedly amended, provided for preservation of significant historical features (buildings, objects, and sites) through a grant in aid program to the States. It established a National Register of Historic Places and a program of matching grants under the existing National Trust for Historic Preservation. As of January 1989, 91 historic sites on national wildlife refuges have been placed on the National Register.

16. National Environmental Policy Act of 1969, as amended (42 U.S.C. 4321-4347).

17. Protection and Enhancement of Environmental Quality Executive Order of 1970 (Executive Order 11514, dated March 5, 1970).

18. Environmental Education Act of 1975 (20 U.S.C. 1531-1536).

19. Use of Off-Road Vehicles on the Public Lands Executive Order of 1972, as amended (Executive Order 11644, dated February 8, 1972, as amended by Executive Order 11989, dated May 24, 1977).

20. Endangered Species Act of 1973 (16 U.S.C. 1531-1543 87 Stat. 884) P.L. 93-205). The Endangered Species Act as amended by Public Law 97-304, The Endangered Species Act Amendments of 1982, dated February 1983.

According to Bean, the 1973 Act "builds its program of protection on three fundamental units. These include two classifications of species--those that are 'endangered' and those that are 'threatened' --and a third classification of geographic areas denominated 'critical habitats.'"[6]

The Act: (1) Authorizes the determination and listing of species as endangered and threatened, and the ranges in which such conditions exist; (2) Prohibits unauthorized taking, possession, sale, and transport of endangered species; (3) Provides authority to acquire land for the conservation of listed species, using land and water conservation funds; (4) Authorizes establishment of cooperative agreements and grants-in-aid to States that establish and maintain active and adequate programs for endangered and threatened wildlife; and, (5) Authorizes the assessment of civil and criminal penalties for violating the Act or regulations.

Section 7 of the Endangered Species Act requires Federal agencies to insure that any action authorized, funded, or carried out by them does not jeopardize the continued existence of listed species or modify their critical habitat.

21. Floodplain Management Executive Order of 1977 (Executive Order 11988, dated May 24, 1977). Wetlands Preservation Executive Order of 1977 (Executive Order 11988, dated May 24, 1977).

These executive orders require both the protection and the enhancement of wetlands and floodplain. Both were signed in May, 1977. When Federally owned wetlands or floodplain are proposed for lease or conveyance to non Federal public or private parties, both executive orders require that the agency: "(a) reference in the conveyance those uses that are restricted under Federal, State or local... regulations; and (b) attach other appropriate restrictions to the uses of such properties by the ... purchaser and any successor, ... or © withhold such properties from..." lease or disposal (E.O. 11990, 4, E.O. 11988, 3(d). In addition, each agency is required to "avoid undertaking or providing assistance" for activities located in wetlands unless (1) ..."there is no practicable alternative...", and (2)... "the proposed action includes all practicable measures to minimize harm...which may result from such use" (E.O. 11990, 2). The term "agency" is defined in both of these executive orders as having the same meaning as the term "Executive agency" which means an Executive department, a Government corporation, and an independent establishment.

[6] Ibid., pp. 331.

22.   The Archaeological Resource Protection Act of 1979 (P.L. 96-95, 93 Sta. 721, dated October 1979). (16 U.S.C. 470aa - 47011).

This Act largely supplanted the resource protection provisions of the Antiquities Act for archaeological items. It established detailed requirements for issuance of permits for any excavation or removal of archaeological resources from Federal or Indian Lands. It also established civil and criminal penalties for the unauthorized excavation, removal, or damage of any such resources; for any trafficking in such resources removed from Federal or Indian land in violation of any provision of Federal law; and for interstate and foreign commerce in such resources acquired, transported, or received in violation of any State or local law. Public Law 100-588, approved November 3, 1988, (102 Stat. 2983) lowered the threshold value of artifacts triggering the felony provision of the Act from $5,000 to $500, made attempting to commit an action prohibited by the Act a violation, and required the land managing agencies to establish public awareness programs regarding the value of archaeological resources to the Nation.

23.   Fish and Wildlife Conservation Act of 1980 (P.L. 96-366, dated September 29, 1980). ("Nongame Act") (16 U.S.C. 2901-2911; 94 Stat. 1322).

Approved September of 1980, this Act authorized grants for development and implementation of comprehensive State nongame fish and wildlife plans and for administration of the Act. It also required the Service to study potential mechanisms for funding these activities and report to Congress by March, 1984. According to Bean, the Act "strives to encourage comprehensive conservation planning, encompassing both nongame and other wildlife...The impetus for the enactment of this legislation was the perception that animals not ordinarily valued for sport hunting or commercial purposes receive insufficient attention and funds from state wildlife management programs."[7]

Public Law 100-653 (102 Stat. 3825), approved November 14, 1988, amended the Act to require the Service to monitor and assess nongame migratory birds, identify those likely to be candidates for endangered species listing, identify appropriate actions, and report to Congress one year from enactment. It also requires the Service to report at five year intervals on actions taken.

24.   Administrative Procedures Act (5 U.S.C. 551-559, 701-706, 1305, 3105, 3344, 4301, 5362, 7521; 60 Stat. 237), as amended (P.L. 79-404, as amended).

25.   Bald Eagle Protection Act of 1940 (16 U.S.C. 668-668d; 54 Stat.), as amended.

26.   Canadian United States Migratory Bird Treaty (Convention Between the United States and Great Britain (for Canada for the Protection of Migratory Birds. (39 Stat. 1702; TS 628), as amended.

27.   Clean Air Act (42 U.S.C. 1857-1857f; 69 Stat. 322), as amended.

28.   Convention on Wetlands of International Importance Especially as Waterfowl Habitats (I.L.M. 11:963-976, September 1972).

This Convention, commonly referred to as the Ramsar Convention, was adopted in Ramsar, Iran, February 3, 1971, and opened for signature at UNESCO headquarters, July 12, 1972. On December 21, 1975, the Convention entered into force after the required signatures of seven countries were obtained. The United Senate consented to ratification of the Convention on October 9, 1986, and the President signed instruments of ratification on November 10, 1986. The Convention maintains a list of wetlands of international importance and works to encourage the wise use of all wetlands in order to preserve the ecological characteristics from which wetland values derive. The Convention is self implementing with the U.S. Fish and Wildlife Service providing U.S. secretariat responsibilities and lead for Convention implementation.

[7] Ibid., pp. 227.

29. Cooperative Research and Training Units Act (16 U.S.C. 753a-753b, 74 Stat. 733), as amended. P.L. 86-686).

30. Federal Aid in Fish Restoration Act (16 U.S.C. 777-777k, 64 Stat. 430).

31. Federal Aid in Wildlife Restoration Act (16 U.S.C. 669-669i; 50 Stat. 917), as amended.

32. Federal Environmental Pesticide Control Act of 1972 (7 U.S.C. 136-136y; 86 Stat. 975), as amended.

33. Federal Land Policy Management Act of 1976 (43 U.S.C. 1701-1771, and other U.S.C. sections; 90 Stat. 2743). Public Law 94-579, October 1976.

34. Federal Property and Administrative Services Act of 1949 (40 U.S.C. 471-535, and other U.S.C. sections; 63 Stat. 378), as amended.

35. Federal Water Pollution Control Act Amendments of 1972 (33 U.S.C. 1251-1265, 1281-1292, 1311-1328, 1341-1345, 1361-1376, and other U.S.C. titles; 86 Stat. 816), as amended.

36. Fish and Wildlife Improvement Act of 1978 (16 U.S.C. 7421; 92 Stat. 3110) P.L. 95-616, November 1978.

37. Flood Control Act of 1944 (16 U.S.C. 460d, 825s and various sections of title 33 and 43 U.S.C.; 58 Stat. 887), as amended and supplemented.

38. Freedom of Information Act (5 U.S.C. 552; 88 Stat. 1561).

39. Refuge Trespass Act (18 U.S.C. 41; Stat 686).

40. Transfer of Certain Real Property for Wildlife Conservation Purposes Act of May 1948, (16 U.S.C. 667b-667d; 62 Stat. 240), as amended.

41. Water Resources Planning Act (42 U.S.C., 1962-1962a-3; 79 Stat. 244), as amended.

42. Waterfowl Depredations Prevention Act (7 U.S.C. 442-445; 70Stat. 492), as amended.

43. Clean Water Act of 1972, Section 404.

    Under this Act, permits are required to be obtained for discharges of dredged and fill materials into all waters, including wetlands. Implementation of the 404 program involves three other federal agencies in addition to limited state involvement. The Environmental Protection Agency (EPA), the National Marine Fisheries Service, and the Service review permit applications and provide comments and recommendations on whether permits should be issued by the Corps. EPA has veto authority over permits involving disposal sites if impacts are considered unacceptable. EPA also develops criteria for discharges and state assumption of the 404 program. Section 404 regulations were changed in 1984 due to a national lawsuit, and 404 jurisdictions now apply to tributaries of navigable waters and isolated wetlands and waters if interstate commerce is involved. With the new regulations, all washes, drainages, and tributaries of navigable waters, including ephemeral and perennial streams, are included under the 404 program in Texas.

44. The Food Security Act of 1985 (Farm Bill).

45. Executive Order 12996. (See page 70)

46. National Wildlife Refuge System Improvement Act of 1997. (See page 71)

Service-Wide Policy Directions

Since the early 1900s, the Service mission and purpose has evolved while holding on to a fundamental national commitment to threatened wildlife ranging from the endangered bison to migratory birds of all types. The earliest national wildlife refuges and preserves are examples of this. Pelican Island, the first refuge, was established in 1903 for the protection of colonial nesting birds such as the snowy egret and the endangered brown pelican. The National Bison Range was instituted for the endangered bison in 1906. Malheur National Wildlife Refuge was established in Oregon in 1908, to benefit all migratory birds with emphasis on colonial nesting species on Malheur Lake. It was not until the 1930s that the focus of refuge programs began to shift toward protection of migratory waterfowl (i.e., ducks and geese). As a result of drought conditions in the 1930s, waterfowl populations became severely depleted. The special emphasis of the Service (then called the Bureau of Sport Fisheries and Wildlife) during the next several decades was on the restoration of critically depleted migratory waterfowl populations.

The passage of the Endangered Species Act of 1973 refocused the activities of the Service as well as other governmental agencies. This Act mandated the conservation of threatened and endangered species of fish, wildlife, and plants both through federal action and by encouraging the establishment of state programs. In the late 1970s, the Bureau of Sport Fisheries and Wildlife was renamed the U.S. Fish and Wildlife Service broadening its scope of wildlife conservation responsibilities to include endangered species as well as game and nongame species. A myriad of other conservation-oriented laws followed, including the Fish and Wildlife Conservation Act of 1980, which emphasized the conservation of nongame species.

The mission of the Fish and Wildlife Service was recently revised by the President of the United States in Executive Order 12996, to reflect the importance of conserving natural resources. The Executive Order states:

> "the mission of the National Wildlife Refuge System is to preserve a national network of lands and waters for the conservation and management of fish, wildlife, and plant resources of the United States for the benefit of present and future generations."

The Executive Order continues by specifying broad guiding principles describing a level of responsibility and concern for the nation's wildlife resources for the ultimate benefit of the people. These principles are as follows:

Public Use
The refuge system provides important opportunities for compatible wildlife-dependent recreational activities involving hunting, fishing, wildlife observation and photography, and environmental education and interpretation.

Habitat
Fish and wildlife will not prosper without high-quality habitat, and without fish and wildlife, traditional uses of refuges cannot be sustained. The refuge system will continue to conserve and enhance the quality and diversity of fish and wildlife habitat within refuges.

Partnerships
America's sportsmen and sportswomen were the first partners who insisted on protecting valuable wildlife habitat within wildlife refuges. Conservation partnerships with other federal agencies, state agencies, tribes, organizations, industry, and the general public can make significant contributions to the growth and management of the refuge system.

Public Involvement
The public should be given a full and open opportunity to participate in decisions regarding acquisition and management of our national wildlife refuges.

The National Wildlife Refuge System Improvement Act of 1997 represents a consensus among diverse constituencies with interests in the management and use of the refuge system. The legislation establishes a strong and singular conservation mission for the National Wildlife Refuge System which is:

> "to administer a national network of lands and waters for the conservation, management, and where appropriate, restoration of the fish, wildlife and plant resources and their habitats with the United States for the benefit of present and future generations of Americans."

In administering the system, the legislation requires the Secretary of the Interior to ensure that the mission of the National Wildlife Refuge System and purposes of the individual refuges are carried out. It also requires the Secretary to maintain the biological integrity, diversity, and environmental health of the refuge system.

The legislation clearly states that each refuge shall be managed to fulfill both the mission of the refuge system and the individual refuge purposes. This serves to underscore that the fundamental mission of the refuge system is wildlife conservation.

The legislation further recognizes wildlife-dependent recreational uses involving hunting, fishing, wildlife observation and photography, and environmental education and interpretation as the priority public uses of the refuge system. These uses are legitimate and appropriate public uses where compatible with the refuge system mission and the individual refuge purposes. These priority public uses are dependent upon healthy wildlife populations, and if the refuges are managed well, these priority public uses will in turn prosper into the future. The legislation also states that these priority public uses receive enhanced consideration over other uses in planning and management.

Scoping and Public Involvement Process

In compliance with the National Environmental Policy Act, community participation continues to be an integral component of the planning for this refuge. Initial planning efforts for the refuge begin in February 1997, with the formation of a team of Service personnel and representatives of several state and local agencies. See Part 1 for a list of participants. A meeting of the team was held to develop a planning strategy and determine methods of involving the public in the planning process.

In April 1997, the Refuge Manager, Jim Krakowski, requested public comments by way of news releases, informational letters, briefings regarding issues, concerns, and opportunities related to the management of the refuge, and personal interviews during public meetings held on March 27 and April 3, 1997. Thus began the process of soliciting public participation to determine the scope of issues to be addressed in planning for the refuge.

To assist individuals and organizations in responding to this request, a survey form was developed and made available. (See Figure 17) The refuge manager received completed surveys and/or letters from numerous individuals and organizations. These survey forms and letters were subsequently analyzed by The Hayden Group, Inc., of Newnan, Georgia, an independent consulting group which provided the Service with a general overview of public opinion regarding management of the refuge.

To enhance public participation during the planning process, a stakeholder group was established in July 1997. The stakeholder group included a broad spectrum of interests offering business, tourism, conservation, recreation, and historical perspectives. See Part 2 for a list of stakeholders. The role of the stakeholder group was to assist in developing the key component of the proposed management plan for the refuge. Stakeholders were selected by the Refuge Manager and through a series of facilitated meetings, all of which were open to anyone wishing to attend, the group utilized key issues, concerns, and opportunities expressed through the survey in drafting its materials. Key components of the proposed plan were consensus tested at community forums held throughout the planning process. Service personnel used all information gathered as a result of the scoping process, the input from the stakeholders, and the series of meetings and community forums held for the stakeholders and the various publics to prepare this draft plan. The meetings occurred as follows:

Workshop #1 - August 12, 1997, Comfort Inn, Naples, Florida

Workshop #2 - September 2, 1997, Comfort Inn, Naples, Florida
      Community Forum #1

Workshop #3 - September 30, 1997, Comfort Inn, Naples, Florida

Workshop #4 - November 5, 1997, Comfort Inn, Naples, Florida
      Community Forum #2

Workshop #5 - December 2, 1997, Comfort Inn, Naples, Florida

All meetings and community forums were facilitated by Jim Stansbury of Stansbury Resolutions by Design, Inc., in Bradenton, Florida.

A mailing list is provided in Part 4.

Figure 19. Survey Form

FLORIDA PANTHER NATIONAL WILDLIFE REFUGE
PUBLIC COMMENT SURVEY FORM

NAME/AFFILIATION_____

ADDRESS_____

CITY/STATE_____ZIP CODE_____

Managed by the U.S. Fish and Wildlife Service (Service), Florida Panther National Wildlife Refuge was established in 1989. The refuge contains approximately 26,400 acres. The refuge forms the core of several panthers' home range and also functions as a travel corridor for panthers traveling between the northern regions of Big Cypress National Preserve and the Fakahatchee Strand State Preserve. During any given month, the refuge may be visited by 5 to 11 different panthers. The refuge was established to provide optimum habitat conditions for the panther and other endangered species.

There are numerous management issues concerning this refuge and the Service would like to hear your opinion on them. We have developed this survey to help you address some of the issues. Please feel free to add additional comments at the end of the form. Your opinions are important and we will use them to help us develop refuge management plans. Thank you for taking the time to provide your comments.

1. Would you like to see more public access to this refuge? _____
If yes, what type of access would you be in favor of?

_____
_____
_____
_____

2. What land use practices do you feel pose a threat to panthers? Do those same practices threaten wetland linkages in southwest Florida watersheds?

_____
_____
_____
_____

3. Would you like to know more about the US Fish and Wildlife Service, the Florida panther, endangered species, prescribed burning, and/or other refuge programs? Please explain.

_____
_____
_____

4. How can the refuge be more effective educating the public about the need to protect the panther and other important natural resources?

_____
_____
_____

5. What concerns/questions do you have that might be addressed through scientific research?

_____
_____
_____
_____

6. Prescribed burning is a land management tool used on the refuge to maintain fire dependent vegetation communities. Do you have any comments on or alternatives to this form of management?

_____
_____
_____
_____
_____

7. Please list any other comments, issues, or concerns you have regarding the refuge. (Add additional sheets if needed)

_____
_____
_____
_____
_____
_____
_____
_____
_____
_____
_____
_____
_____
_____
_____
_____
_____

Part 1 - Participants

David Addison - The Conservancy of Southwest Florida, Naples, Florida
Ken Alvarez - Florida Park Service, Osprey, Florida
Jim Brown - Fish and Wildlife Service, Atlanta, Georgia
Frank Cole - Fish and Wildlife Service, Tallahassee, Florida
Kim Dryden - Florida Game and Freshwater Fish Commission, Punta Gorda, Florida
Dave Erickson - Fish and Wildlife Service, Atlanta, Georgia
Fesseha Gebremikael - Fish and Wildlife Service, Atlanta, Georgia
Jennifer Harris, Fish and Wildlife Service, Atlanta, Georgia
Rick Kanaski - Fish and Wildlife Service, Savannah Coastal Refuges, Savannah, Georgia
Jim Krakowski - Florida Panther National Wildlife Refuge
Mike Mayer - Everglades National Park, Everglades City, Florida
Wendell Metzen - Fish and Wildlife Service, Jacksonville, Florida
Ananta Nath - South Florida Water Management District
Ben Nottingham - Florida Panther National Wildlife Refuge
Mike Owen - Fakahatchee Strand State Preserve, Copeland, Florida
Jon Staiger - City of Naples, Naples, Florida
Chris Straton - Collier County Audubon Society, Naples, Florida
Kris Thoemke - Florida Wildlife Federation, Naples, Florida
Jerry Vits - Fish and Wildlife Service, Atlanta, Georgia

Part 2 - Stakeholders

Ken Alvarez -	Florida Park Service
Fred Barfield -	Private Landowner
Ilene Barnett -	Florida Department of Environmental Protection
Ed Carlson -	Corkscrew Swamp Sanctuary National Audubon Society
Ron Clark -	Big Cypress National Preserve
Brad Cornell -	Collier County Conservation Club, Friends of the Florida Panther
John DiNunzio -	Collier County Conservation Club, Friends of the Florida Panther
Roger Dykstra -	Orchards and Egrets Eco-tours
Wally Hibbard -	Alternate: Big Cypress National Preserve
Bill Lorenz -	Collier County Natural Resources Department
Ray March -	Land Manager for Private Landowner
Jim McMullen -	Alternate for Roger Dykstra
Skip Riffle -	Bass Anglers
Jim Schortemeyer -	Florida Game and Fresh Water Fish Commission
Ed Schuppenhauer -	Alternate for Fran Stallings
Michael Simonik -	Conservancy of Southwest Florida
Fran Stallings -	Environmental Coalition of Southwest Florida
Clarence Tears -	South Florida Water Management District - Big Cypress Basin
Kris Thoemke -	Florida Wildlife Federation

Part 3 - Service Responses to Issues, Concerns, and Opportunities

The following topics were identified by the Service and through the public involvement process. Comments listed are representative of those received by the Service; responses from the Service follow the comments.

1. Access to the Refuge

The refuge has been closed to public access except for limited, small group tours. This was by far the biggest issue during the planning process for the refuge. Comments ranged the full spectrum, from maintaining the refuge as an inviolate sanctuary to proposals for multi-recreational pursuits.

Issues, Concerns, and Opportunities Regarding Access:

- Survey responses were split: 50 percent wanted more access; 50 percent did not
- Allow a limited-hunter deer and turkey hunt
- Allow sport fishing on Colding and Pistol ponds
- Establish hiking trails and camping opportunities
- Adjacent public areas allow multiple public use - keep the refuge an inviolate sanctuary
- Allow foot access only
- Provide more tours or interpretive trails
- Allow off-road vehicle use
- Need for bird watching and photography areas
- Refuge was established for panthers, increasing public use or harvesting panther prey will violate refuge purpose

Stakeholder Consensus and Recommendations Regarding Access:
Except for an interpretive foot trail, <u>disallow</u> any new public uses at the start. Within a 5-year period, use research to evaluate hunting, fishing, hiking, camping and other potential uses to determine if they are compatible with the purpose of the refuge.

Service Responses Regarding Access:
Before allowing any secondary use to occur on a national wildlife refuge, the Service must consider first and foremost the purpose of the refuge. This refuge was established to provide habitat for the endangered Florida panther. The panther is the most endangered large animal in existence in the United States. Because of this critical endangered status, management decisions must be oriented towards providing optimum conditions for the panther. We must also consider what effects these secondary uses may potentially have upon management and research activities that are presently occurring on the refuge or being proposed for the refuge.

For example, studies underway involve the radio instrumentation of deer, which requires an extensive amount of time and resources to catch and monitor the animals. We have found that deer are very hard to catch and collar in the wooded swamps of south Florida. Data from multiple animals of various sex and age classes are needed over several years. The loss of one of these radio-collared deer to a hunt-related incident could have drastic implications to the study. Moreover, because the refuge is the only publicly owned area that receives heavy panther use and is not open to public access and hunting, it has been used as a "control site" (non-hunting area) for ongoing and/or planned studies to evaluate what impact human activities (i.e., other sites such as Big Cypress National Preserve) have on the panther.

Some of the potential uses (hunting and fishing) are of the type that have been promoted as priority uses for refuges in general by recent directives and acts. However, because of the panther's critical status and purpose for which this refuge was established, we must be very cautious. If we are to err, in terms of the nature and extent of allowed use, it must be in favor of the panther. The Service agrees with the recommendations of the stakeholder committee except for the amount of time it may take to make decisions. The stakeholder committee felt that in five years a decision should be made on each of the other potential uses. The Service will review the program in five years, but decisions may take place before or after that date depending on the results of studies and monitoring. Most of this research will be contracted out to universities. The Service cannot predict whether or not studies will be funded, occur in a timely manner, or if the research will produce the results needed to make decisions.

The Service does believe that some limited access can occur on this refuge and proposes the following to be developed as soon as funding and permitting processes can be completed. First, the construction of a short interpretive trail in the southeast corner of the refuge; second, the construction of a waterbird viewing area along SR 29. Both would be placed in areas of least use by panthers, would not adversely affect the animals, and would serve to enlighten people of their plight and other resources of the refuge. These projects would also include educational signs informing and promoting refuge programs.

Research projects (i.e., 24-hour panther monitoring) needed to make compatibility decisions require funding and technology that may not be available within the time frame suggested.

2. Cooperative Land Management and Partnerships Within the Big Cypress Watershed

Repeatedly during the scoping process, it was pointed out that the refuge was one of many public land management entities which, along with private land interests, make up the Big Cypress Watershed and that management actions in one part of the watershed may have adverse impacts to other parts of the system. Many comments favored the cooperative management of the entire watershed to ensure the protection of hydrologic, ecological, and environmental values of the system.

Issues, Concerns, and Opportunities Regarding Cooperative Land Management and Partnerships within the Big Cypress Watershed:

- Land use affecting water flow poses a threat to panthers
- Land development and agriculture pose a threat to panthers
- Protect panther corridors
- Development and agriculture tend to threaten wetland linkages within the watershed
- Habitat fragmentation is occurring within the headwaters of the watershed on privately owned lands
- Public lands are not managed as well as private lands
- There is no coordination among the land management entities, both public and private

Stakeholder Consensus and Recommendations Regarding Cooperative Land Management and Partnerships within the Big Cypress Watershed:

The group, as a whole, recognized how important this issue was and actually drafted Goal 4.0 for the plan, which is, "Promote interagency and private landowner cooperation for the management of natural and cultural resources within the Big Cypress Watershed."

Service Responses Regarding Cooperative Land Management and Partnerships within the Big Cypress Watershed:

The Service agrees with the recommendations of the stakeholder committee. More communication and coordination with the other land managers within the watershed must occur if we are to effectively conserve the diverse resources of this ecosystem. The plan outlines steps needed to improve this coordination and the Service will take the lead in this effort.

3. Public Awareness of the Panther and Refuge Programs

Almost all of the survey respondents indicated they would like to know more about the panther and refuge programs. Because the refuge is closed to public access and lacks a visitor contact station at the refuge, it is difficult to provide this needed information to the public. The recovery of the panther and success of the refuge program will depend upon an informed public ready to support a sustainable environment.

Issues, Concerns, and Opportunities Regarding Public Awareness of the Panther and Refuge Programs:

■ Almost all respondents wanted more information
■ Most of the survey respondents suggested that staff should give school programs
■ Give more refuge tours and allow access to learn about refuge programs
■ Use mass media to get the information to a broader base
■ Use volunteers and support groups to help disseminate the information
■ Establish a speakers' bureau for groups and public functions
■ Expand public outreach programs
■ Establish a web site on the Internet with panther and refuge-specific information

Stakeholder Responses Regarding Public Awareness of the Panther and Refuge Programs:

The group recognized the importance of this issue by fully supporting and assisting with the drafting of Goal 3.0, "Increase local awareness of the South Florida Ecosystem, the refuge, and the Florida panther through the development and implementation of an outreach program by 2003."

Service Responses Regarding Public Awareness of the Panther and Refuge Programs:

In order to recover the panther and protect the other resources of the refuge and the South Florida Ecosystem, the public must be informed of the issues at hand and conservation efforts that are needed. The Service agrees with the stakeholder committee that significant changes are needed to enhance the environmental education program on the refuge. These changes are reflected in the strategies of the plan where additional staff will be asked to inform the public of the environmental status and needs of southwest Florida.

4. Protect Panther Habitat on Private Lands - Protection Through Less Than Fee Simple Acquisition

Approximately half of the habitat used by the panther is in private ownership. These private lands contain a greater percentage of upland habitats and soils consisting of greater nutrient value which tend to support healthier panthers. Most of the private landowners are not interested in selling their lands for panther conservation, yet a few of them would be interested in maintaining some areas in natural landscapes. However, they are inclined to seek at least some income off the land just to help pay annual taxes on these lands. Many want to pass their property to their offspring, but fear a large inheritance tax. The solution is to protect these habitats through conservation easements, tax breaks, mitigation banks, or some type of monetary incentive for the landowner to keep important panther habitat in its natural state.

Issues, Concerns, and Opportunities Regarding the Protection of Panther Habitat on Private Lands - Protection Through Less Than Fee Simple Acquisition:

• Loss of panther habitat to development is the biggest threat to panthers
• Cattle ranching that emphasizes native range is not a serious problem
• Private landowners are managing their areas better than the public agencies, that is why they hold more game and panthers
• Tax incentives and conservation easements are viable alternatives to fee simple purchase
• The increasing southwest Florida human population will increase habitat and people pressure problems

Stakeholder Consensus and Recommendations Regarding the Protection of Panther Habitat on Private Lands - Protection Through Less Than Fee Simple Acquisition:

When a subgroup of the committee reviewed Goal 4.0, they felt that Objective 4.3, "Inform and assist private landowners with federal cooperative programs that will enhance or protect wildlife habitat," was the most important objective listed under this goal. The committee agreed with the subgroup's analysis.

Service Responses Regarding Protection of Panther Habitat on Private Lands - Protection Through Less Than Fee Simple Acquisition:

Loss of habitat is a principal reason the panther is endangered today. If this trend continues, the panther will be lost tomorrow. Habitat important to the panther is also critical to many other plants and animals. These areas benefit humans by being flood retention areas, water filters and drinking water recharge zones. However, many of the large landowners of important panther habitat in southwest Florida have indicated no desire to sell their land to the government. Ways must be found, however, to conserve this habitat. The stakeholders have identified this issue and we agree with their conclusion. The Service will pursue a program with willing landowners of important panther habitat to initiate a conservation easement program.

5. Visitor Center and Interpretive Facilities

Many people thought that a visitor center was needed to inform people about the panther, the recovery effort, and refuge management programs. There have been discussions between state and federal agencies about locating a multi-agency visitor center on state property in the southwest corner of the I-75 and SR 29 intersection, adjacent to the refuge. The area has been disturbed as it was used as a rock quarry site for road base material. The site is covered with invasive exotic plants. An interpretive foot trail extending into the refuge could begin and end at this location.

Issues, Concerns and Opportunities Regarding a Visitor Center and Interpretive Facilities:

- Visitor Center is needed to inform the public about the panther and refuge activities
- After a narrative video, provide a vehicular tour of the refuge
- Provide a facility that school groups can come to and learn about the panther
- Construct an interpretive facility somewhere along SR 29
- Set aside a small educational site near the headquarters for school groups and visitors
- Additional staffing needed for education
- Take advantage of the millions passing by on I-75
- Be careful not to construct facilities in a wetland or in vital habitat for the panther or other endangered species

Stakeholder Consensus and Recommendations Regarding a Visitor Center and Interpretive Facilities:

On November 5, 1997, the committee voted unanimously that a Visitor Center be constructed close to the I-75 corridor, be a multi-agency venture, and not on a site containing sensitive resources. It could be located either inside or outside the refuge.

Service Responses Regarding a Visitor Center and Interpretive Facilities:

The I-75 highway connects Naples to Miami and bisects the greatest wetlands of the United States, the Everglades and Big Cypress Swamp. Yet, no facility exists along this stretch to fully inform the public of the wonders of these wetlands or the major restoration events that are taking place. No site exists where school groups can go and learn about the dynamics of this intricate system. The SR 29 and I-75 interchange offers a perfect venue for a multi-agency visitor center and environmental center to accomplish these endeavors. The Service agrees with the stakeholder group about the importance of such a facility and has included strategies in the plan to pursue the installation of a visitor center and environmental education classroom.

6. Refuge Research and Management
Responses received indicated that research projects and habitat management were important endeavors that needed to be continued. It was also evident that most of the public was not aware of what activities were occurring on the refuge. Most of the respondents understood that prescribed burning was a management tool needed to maintain fire dependent communities. Only two comments expressed some concern about prescribed burning.

Issues, Concerns, and Opportunities Regarding Refuge Research and Management:
- Research needs to address water runoff from agriculture fields
- Studies and monitoring needed on drainage and hydroperiod changes within the watershed
- Nutrients/Contaminants in the watershed need to be monitored
- Panther health issues and secondary impacts of water-borne contaminants (especially mercury)
- Methods of increasing/strengthening the panther population
- Continue research on prescribed fire
- Study the impacts of human activity on panthers
- More knowledge is needed on panther habitat, habits, and movement
- Activity monitoring of panthers on a 24-hour basis

Stakeholder Consensus and Recommendations Regarding Refuge Research and Management:
The committee reviewed and helped draft the various refuge research objectives that are included in the plan. The committee wholeheartedly supports past and present research and habitat management efforts and those suggested in the plan.

Service Responses Regarding Refuge Research and Management:
This research will always be an important function of the refuge. Priority will be placed on applied panther research, or studies that will provide information to assist in the management of panthers or their habitats. The refuge should serve as a center for applied science and management information for other agencies and private landowners. The Service agrees with the stakeholder committee on the importance of this issue and we have addressed its importance through strategies in the plan.

Bio-medical evaluation conducted on captured Florida panther
USFWS photo by Larry W. Richardson

7. Lack of Adequate Refuge Staffing
The refuge was established in 1989, and is a young refuge. It was developed during a period of austere budgets and federal government downsizing. The plan recognizes this fact and describes new initiatives that are needed to successfully address the Service responsibilities for the refuge and the South Florida Ecosystem over the next 15 years. These initiatives include an expanded public education and outreach program; increased coordination with land managers off the refuge and the initiation of a conservation easement program for important panther habitats; an enhanced

biological and habitat monitoring program; and expanded management program for flora, fauna, and the public. The plan identifies the following new positions for the refuge complex, which includes Ten Thousand Islands National Wildlife Refuge: private lands biologist, media specialist, easement biologist, geographic information system specialist, hydrologist, assistant manager, public use specialist, auto mechanic, maintenance worker, and an administrative assistant.

Issues, Concerns, and Opportunities Regarding Lack of Adequate Refuge Staffing:

- Cannot accomplish all of these new initiatives with existing staff
- Use volunteers to help with the initiatives
- Coordinate more with other agencies to pool resources
- Don't need all of this government intervention, let nature take its course

Stakeholder Consensus and Recommendations Regarding Lack of Adequate Refuge Staffing:

The committee recognized that lack of staff was an issue for the refuge at present and for the new initiatives outlined in the plan. The committee helped draft the objectives of the plan that identified the need for additional staff.

Service Responses Regarding Lack of Adequate Refuge Staffing:

The refuge is located within the center of the Big Cypress Watershed and will play a pivotal role in the success of ecosystem protection and restoration initiatives in southwest Florida. The plan outlines many new initiatives for this young refuge. The Services agrees with the stakeholder committee that additional staff is needed to carry out the plan and will support the strategies described to fill these positions. Volunteer assistance will also be sought through the existing "Friends Group" and other support groups.

8. Oil and Gas Exploration

The Service does not own the refuge subsurface mineral rights. Most of the ownership lies within various Collier interests. In November 1997, the Collier Resource Company submitted a "Plan of Operations" to conduct seismic and exploratory well activities on the refuge. This is the first time the refuge has had to coordinate and manage this type of activity. The exploration is scheduled to occur in 1998 and thereafter.

Issues, Concerns, and Opportunities Regarding Oil and Gas Exploration:

- The Service needs to acquire the mineral rights to protect the surface resources
- A plan is needed to coordinate and minimize adverse surface impacts of any exploration activity
- Slant drilling off the refuge should be utilized to protect the panther and refuge resources
- The Comprehensive Conservation Plan should address mineral rights and exploration

Stakeholder Consensus and Recommendations Regarding Oil and Gas Exploration:

The committee recognized the importance of this issue and supported the drafting of Objective 2.1, "Minimize the impact from oil and gas exploration and extraction on the refuge."

Service Responses Regarding Oil and Gas Exploration:

The Service supports the stakeholder recommendation on refuge oil and gas activities. All care must be taken to minimize adverse impacts to the panther and other refuge surface resources. Acquisition of subsurface mineral rights is difficult and expensive, however, all alternatives will definitely be explored to protect this important environmental area.

Part 4 - Mailing List

Jack Abney
82 Johnnycake Drive
Naples, Florida 34110

Franklin Adams
Izaak Walton League of America
4272 19th Place, SW.
Naples, Florida 33999

Dave Addison
The Conservancy of Southwest
Florida
1450 Merrihue
Naples, Florida 34102

Ken Alvarez
Southwest Florida Parks
District IV, Administration
1843 Tamiami Trail
Osprey, Florida 34229

Bob Baker
24340 Sandpiper Isle Way, #803
Bonita Springs, Florida 34134-2992

Pam Ball
P.O. Box 575
Goodland, Florida 34140

Fred Barfield
P.O. Box 3265
Immokalee, Florida 34143

Ilene Barnett
Florida Department of
Environmental Protection
2295 Victoria Avenue, Suite 364
Ft. Myers, Florida 33901

Gary Beardsley
Environmental Consultant
2396 13th Street North
Naples, Florida 33940

Barbara Berry
Board of Commissioners
3301 Tamiami Trail
Naples, Florida 34113

James Billie, Chairman
Seminole Tribe of Florida
6703 Steirling Road
Hollywood, Florida 33024

Maureen Bonness
7390 Rookery Lane
Naples, Florida 34120

Buddy W. Bunker
Sprint/United Telephone Company
P.O. Box 2477
Naples, Florida 33962

Clyde Butcher
Big Cypress Gallery
52388 Tamiami Trail, East
Ochopee, Florida 33943

Ed Carlson
Corkscrew Swamp
Audubon Sanctuary
375 Sanctuary Road, W.
Naples, Florida 34120

Jasper Carlton
Biodiversity Legal Foundation
Box 18327
Boulder, Colorado 80308

Roy Cawley, Vice President
Collier Enterprises, Inc.
3003 North Tamiami Trail
Naples, Florida 33940

Ron Clark, Superintendent
Wallace Hibbard
Big Cypress National Preserve
SR Box 110
Ochopee, Florida 34141

Dottie Cook
Southwest Florida Regional
Planning Council
P.O. Box 3455
North Fort Myers, Florida 33918

Brad Cornell
Collier County Audubon
556 109th Avenue, North
Naples, Florida 34108

Jeff Cox, Lieutenant
Collier County Sheriff's
Department
3301 E. Tamiami Trail
Naples, Florida 33962

Robert Curry
121 23rd Street, NW.
Naples, Florida

Billy Cypress, Chairman
Miccosukee Tribe
P.O. Box 440021, Tamiami Station
Miami, Florida 33144

Wayne Daltry
South Florida Regional
Planning Council
4980 Dayline Drive, 4th Floor
North Ft. Myers, Florida 33917

Woodrow Darden
Florida Game and Fresh Water
Fish Commission
551 North Military Trail
West Palm Beach, Florida 33415

Tony Davis
Davis 7 Associates
P.O. Box 7488
Naples, Florida 33941

Frank Denninger
461 East 40th Street
Hialeah, Florida 33013

Frank DiAndriole
Betty DiAndriole
434 Wiggins Lake Court, #101
Naples, Florida 34110

John DiNunzio
1279 29th Street, SW.
Naples, Florida 34117

John Drury
Collier County Airport Authority
2800 N. Horseshoe Drive
Naples, Florida 33942

Kim Dryden
Florida Game and Fresh Water
Fish Commission
29200 Tucker's Grade
Punta Gorda, Florida

Fred Dudley, State Senator
1718 Cape Coral Parkway East
Cape Coral, Florida 33904

Sonja Durrwachter
Florida Division of Forestry
710 Randall Boulevard
Naples, Florida 34120

Roger Dykstra
Orchids and Egrets
238 Siverado Drive
Naples, Florida 34119

Jim Goodwin
South Florida Water
Management District
2301 McGregor Boulevard
Ft. Myers, Florida 33901

Robert Gore
P.O. Box 10053
Naples, Florida 34101

Porter Goss, Congressman
2000 Main Street, Suite 407
Ft. Myers, Florida 33901

Bob Graham, Senator
241 Dirksen Senate Office Building
Washington, DC 20510

Joan Griffin
Joan's Kwick Stop Country Store
39395 Tamiami Trail, East
Ochopee, Florida 33943

David Guggenheim
The Conservancy of
Southwest Florida
1450 Merrihue
Naples, Florida 34102

Ed Hall
Sprint/United Telephone
P.O. Box 2477
Naples, Florida 33939

Harold Hall
1082 Rainbow Drive
Naples, Florida 33942

Tim Hancock, Chairman
Board of Commissioners
3301 Tamiami Trail
Naples, Florida 34113

Robert Henry, Manager
Collier Seminole State Park
20200 Tamiami Trail East
Naples, Florida 34114

Richard Hilsenbeck
The Nature Conservancy
515-A North Adams Street
Talahassee, FL 32301

Lou Hinds, Refuge Manager
Ding Darling National
Wildlife Refuge
1 Wildlife Drive
Sanibel, Florida 33957

Bob Hoch
20561 Porthole Court
Estero, Florida 33928

Daryl Hughes
520 27th Street, NW.
Naples, Florida

Pat Humphries
441 20 Avenue, NW.
Naples, Florida

Kenneth Jenne, State Senator
110 Southeast 6th Street, 9th Floor
Ft. Lauderdale, Florida 33301

Holly Jensen
11714 SW 89 Street
Gainesville, Florida 32608-6289

Bonnie Kelley
12417 NE 7 Avenue
Gainesville, Florida 32641

Ellier Krier
NACC/EDC Coalition for
Government and
Community Affairs
3620 N. Tamiami Trail
Naples, Florida 33940

Colleen Kvetko
Fifth Avenue Bank of Florida
4099 Tamiami Trail, North
Naples, Florida 33940

Charles Lee
Florida Audubon
1101 Audubon Way
Maitland, Florida 32751

Ross Longmire, Division
Manager
Barron Collier Company
2600 Golden Gate Parkway,
Suite 200
Naples, Florida 33942-3206

William Lorenz
Collier County Natural Resources
3301 East Tamiami Trail
Naples, Florida 34112

Gary Lytton
Rookery Bay National
Estuarine Reserve
300 Tower Road
Naples, Florida 34113

Connie Mack, Senator
517 Hart Senate Office Building
Washington, DC 20510

Sidney Maddock
Box 1359
Buxton, North Carolina 27920

Ray March
Collier Enterprises
P.O. Box 1115
Immokalee, Florida 34143

Brian Marsh
1450 Merrihue Drive
Naples, Florida 34139

Tammie Mathews
Visit Naples, Inc.
3620 N. Tamiami Trail
Naples, Florida 34102

Bettye Matthews
Board of Commissioners
3301 Tamiami Trail, East
Naples, Florida 33962

Lynn McMillen
Smallwood Store
P.O. Box 367
Chokoloskee, Florida 33925

Jim McMullen
3014 44th Avenue, SW.
Naples, Florida 34116

Don Metcalf
Barb Metcalf
1090 Egret's Walk Circle, #101
Naples, Florida 34108

Chuck Mohlke
Fraser and Mohlke, Inc.
P.O. Box 2312
Naples, Florida 33939

Jack Moller
610 27th Street, SW.
Pembroke Pines, Florida 33024

Bill Monarchino
4735 Via Carmen
Naples, Florida 34105

Sonny Mowbry
RR1, Box 4
LaBelle, Florida 33935

William O'Neill
Buckingham, Doolittle & Burroughs
5551 Ridgewood Drive
Naples, Florida 33963

Curtis Ogden
1483 San Marco Boulevard
Naples, Florida

John M. Passidomo
Cheffy, Passidomo,
Wilson & Johnson
821 Fifth Avenue, South
Naples, Florida 33940

Pat Pelican
Right Choice
277 North Collier Boulevard
Marco Island, Florida 33937

Pat Pilcher
Izaack Walton League
257 Seabreeze Avenue
Naples, Florida 33963

Tony Polizos
Agriculture Center
14700 Immokalee Road
Naples, Florida 33964

Ronnie Poplock
5993 3rd Street, N.
Naples, Florida

Barbara Powell
Everglades Protection Society, Inc.
22951 SW 190 Avenue
Miami, Florida 33170

Oannes Pritzer
1731 16th Avenue, NE.
Naples, Florida 33964

Marney Reed
12425 Union Road
Naples, Florida 34114-9626

Skip Riffle
5950 Cope Lane
Naples, Florida 34112

Allan Rigerman
17910 NW 84th Avenue
Hialeah, Florida 33015-2605

Richard Ring, Superintendent
Everglades National Park
P.O. Box 279
Homestead, Florida 33030

Mark Robson
Florida Game and Fresh Water
Fish Commission
551 North Military Trail
West Palm Beach, Florida 33415

Luis Rojas, State Representative
3301 East Tamiami Trail, Suite 305
Naples, Florida 34113

Robert H. Roth
Silver Strand Division
Barron Collier Company
P.O. Drawer K
Immokalee, Florida 33934

Nicole Ryan
The Conservancy of
Southwest Florida
1450 Merrihue
Naples, Florida 34102

Burt Saunders, State
Representative
3301 Tamiami Trail
Naples, Florida 34113

Brian Scherf
1060 Tyler
Hollywood, Florida 33019

Jim Schortemeyer
Florida Game and Fresh Water
Fish Commission
566 Commercial Boulevard
Naples, Florida 33942

Ed Schuppenhauer
Bop 8776
Naples, Florida 34101

Mike Shirley
Rookery Bay National
Estuarine Reserve
300 Tower Road
Naples, Florida 34113

Mike Simonik
The Conservancy of
Southwest Florida
1450 Merrihue
Naples, Florida 34139

JoAnn Smallwood
Smallwood Design Group
6901 Airport Road, North
Naples, Florida 33942

Nancy Smith
1161 27th Street, SW.
Naples, Florida 34117

Alexander Sprunt
Audubon Regional Office
115 Indian Mound Trail
Tavernier, Florida 33070

Jon Staiger, Manager
Naples City Hall
735 8th Street, South
Naples, Florida 34102

Fran Stallings, Ph.D.
Box 8776
Naples, Florida 34101-8776

Robert Steiger, Manager
Delnor Wiggins State Park
11100 Gulfshore Drive North
Naples, Florida 34108

Sheilah Stobei
Chokoloskee Island Park
P.O. Box 430
Chokoloskee, Florida 33925

Chris Straton
Collier County Audubon Society
P.O. Box 797
Naples, Florida 34101

Joe Taksel
ARFF
P.O. Box 841154
Pembroke Pines, Florida 33084

Clarence Tears
Big Cypress Basin Water
Management
6167 Janes Lane
Naples, Florida 33943

Kris Thoemke
Florida Wildlife Federation
5051 Castello Drive, Suite 240
Naples, Florida 34103

Gregg Toppin, Manager
Fakahatchee Strand State Preserve
P.O. Box 548
Copeland, Florida 34137

Lee Treadwell
Barron Collier Company
2640 Golden Gate Parkway
Naples, Florida 34105

Kaydee Tuff
Tuff Publications, Inc.
2301 CR 951, Unit C
Naples, Florida 33999

Mike Tussey
2527 44th Avenue, SW.
Naples, Florida 34116

Roberta Vallery
180 Cypress Way
Naples, Florida 34110

Frank Vautrot
Big Cypress Wilderness Institute
HCR 61, Box 177
Copeland, Florida 33926

Ginger Westman
League of Women Voters
116 Bond Court
Marco Island, Florida 33937

Steve Williams
Florida Panther Society
Route 1, Box 1895
White Springs, Florida 32096

Gene Wooten
Wooten's Airboat Tours
Star Route, Box 121
Ochopee, Florida 33943

Raymond R. Wooten
U.S. 41, Tamiami Trail
Ochopee, Florida 33943

Draft Interim Compatibility Determination

Use:
- Increased access for wildlife observation and environmental education;
- New strategies for study and management as detailed in the attached Draft Florida Panther Comprehensive Conservation Plan of 1998.

Station Name:
Florida Panther National Wildlife Refuge

Date Established:
June 21, 1989

Establishing and Acquisition Authorities:
16 U.S.C. 1534 (Endangered Species Act of 1973)
16 U.S.C. 742f(a)(4) (Fish and Wildlife Act of 1956)
16 U.S.C. 742f(b)(1) (Fish and Wildlife Act of 1956)

Purposes for which the Refuge was Established:
- "...conserve (A) fish and wildlife which are listed as endangered or threatened species... or (B) plants...." (Endangered Species Act 1973)

- "...for the development, advancement, management, conservation, and protection of fish and wildlife resources...."(Fish and Wildlife Act of 1956)

- "...for the benefit of the Fish and Wildlife Service, in performing its activities and services. Such acceptance may be subject to the terms of any restrictive or affirmative covenant, or condition of servitude...." (Fish and Wildlife Act of 1956)

- "...for the benefit and recovery of the endangered Florida panther...." (Fish and Wildlife Service "Fakahatchee Strand Environmental Assessment of 1985")

- "...Florida Panther National Wildlife Refuge is essential to the survival of the panther and the refuge should enhance habitat conditions for the panther and use programs designed to increase the carrying capacity for deer, a major prey resource...." (Fish and Wildlife Service "Florida Panther Recovery Plan of 1995")

Refuge Goals:
1.0 Provide optimum habitat conditions for the Florida panther with special consideration for other endangered and threatened species.
2.0 Restore and conserve the natural diversity, abundance, and ecological function of refuge flora and fauna.
3.0 Develop and implement an educational program that will provide an understanding and appreciation of the Florida panther, fish and wildlife ecology, and human influence on ecosystems of south Florida.
4.0 Promote interagency and private landowner cooperation for the management of natural and cultural resources within the Big Cypress Watershed.
5.0 Protect refuge cultural resources in accordance with federal and state historic preservation legislation and regulations.
6.0 Provide opportunities for compatible public use in accordance with the National Wildlife Refuge System Improvement Act of 1997.

In addition, follow the Goals of the National Wildlife Refuge System (Attachment 1).

Other Applicable Laws, Regulations and Policies:

National Wildlife Refuge Administration Act of 1966 as amended (16 USC 668dd-668ee).
Antiquities Act of 1906 (34 Stat. 225).
Refuge Recreation Act of 1962 (16 USC 460k-460k-4).
Title 50; Code of Federal Regulations; Parts 25-33.
Migratory Bird Treaty Act of 1918 (15 USC 703-711).
Bald and Golden Eagle Protection Act (16 USC 41).
National Environmental Policy Act of 1969, NEPA (42 USC 4321).
Refuge Revenue Sharing Act of 1935 (16 USC 715s).
Criminal Code Provisions of 1940 (18 USC 41).
Refuge Trespass Act of June 25, 1948 (18 USC 41; 62 Stat. 686).
National Historic Preservation Act of 1966 (16 USC 470).
National Wildlife Refuge Regulations for the most recent year (50 CFR Subchptr C; 43 CFR 3101.3-3).
North American Wetlands Conservation Act of 1990.
Management and General Public Use of the National Wildlife Refuge System, Executive Order 12996, March 25, 1996.
National Wildlife Refuge System Administrative Act of 1997.

The following refuge specific Management Plans: Fire Plan, Wildlife Inventory Plan, Hurricane Action Plan, and Law Enforcement Plan all have been approved by the Fish and Wildlife Service Southeast Regional Office.

Additional refuge specific regulations as published.

Description of Use:

A. Increase in human access to the refuge for wildlife observation and environmental education. Specifically, the following measures will be developed.

■ Construction of a ½ to ¾ mile interpretive foot trail. The trail will be placed in an area of least use by panthers. The trail would contain interpretive and educational exhibits on refuge programs and the plight of the panther. The trail would be day-use only. Interpretive exhibits would be installed along the trail. Parking and restroom facilities would be provided at the trailhead.

■ A waterbird and other wildlife viewing area adjacent to SR29. This project includes the development of a parking area, restroom facilities, interpretive exhibits, and observation decks. The wildlife viewing area would be day-use only.

■ The development and use of a multi-agency visitor center and environmental education center adjacent to the SR29 and I-75 interchange or along the SR29 corridor.

B. The 1998 Draft Comprehensive Conservation Plan for Florida Panther National Wildlife Refuge contains six refuge goals. Each goal has new strategies for study and management.

These uses are further defined in the Draft Comprehensive Conservation Plan and appended Environmental Assessment.

Anticipated Biological Impacts of the Use:

It is not anticipated that such activities will have major adverse effects on the panther or other refuge flora and fauna. The impacts of these activities are more fully described in the attached Draft Comprehensive Conservation Plan/Environmental Assessment. This compatibility determination is based on the findings and recommendations of that plan.

NEPA Compliance:

_____ Categorical Exclusion

_XX_ Environmental Assessment

_____ Environmental Impact Statement

_XX_ Finding of No Significant Impact

Determination: (Check One)

_XX_ This use is compatible.

_____ This use is not compatible.

Stipulations Necessary to Ensure Compatibility:

All of the activities discussed within the Draft Comprehensive Conservation Plan for Florida Panther National Wildlife Refuge will be considered compatible with the purposes of the refuge if guidelines provided in the plan are followed as prescribed. If there is any evidence which indicates such activities create adverse impacts, the activity will cease or be curtailed.

Justification:

A. Access. Wildlife observation and environmental education are important secondary uses as they create an awareness of our resources and the problems facing management. These uses will help educate the public on the plight of the panther. The status of the panther is in a critical state and increased awareness is desperately needed.

B. Studies and Management. The studies and techniques outlined in the attached plan have been designed to better facilitate management of the natural systems on and off the refuge.

Submitted
by:_____
Project Leader   Date

Reviewed
by:_____
District Manager   Date

Approved
by:_____
GARD, Area III   Date
Refuges and Wildlife, Atlanta, GA

Attachment 1
Goals Of The National Wildlife Refuge System

1. To preserve, restore and enhance in their natural ecosystems (when practicable) all species of animals and plants that are endangered or threatened with becoming endangered.

2. To perpetuate the migratory bird resource.

3. To preserve a natural diversity and abundance of flora and fauna.

4. To provide an understanding and appreciation of fish and wildlife ecology and humanity's role in environment, and to provide refuge visitors with high quality, safe, wholesome and enjoyable recreational experiences oriented toward wildlife to the extent these activities are compatible with the purpose(s) for which the refuge was established.

Draft Intra-Service Section 7 Consultation

Division/Office: U.S. Fish and Wildlife Service, Florida Panther National Wildlife Refuge

Project Biologist/Phone Number: Jim Krakowski /(941) 353-8442 ext. 27

Date: April 8, 1998

I. **Proposed Action:**
Activities associated with the 1998 Comprehensive Conservation Plan for Florida Panther National Wildlife Refuge. The Plan would increase access to the refuge and implement additional study and management projects.

II. **Location (County and State/attach project area map):**
Collier County, Florida

III. **Description of proposed action (describe in enough detail to allow proper evaluation of project impacts, attach additional pages as needed):**
Action can be divided into two major areas:

A. **Increase in human access to the refuge for wildlife observation and environmental education.** Specifically, the following measures will be developed.

(1) Construction of a ½ to ¾ mile interpretive foot trail. The trail will be placed in an area of least use by panthers. The trail would contain interpretive and educational exhibits on refuge programs and the plight of the panther. The trail would be day-use only. Interpretive exhibits would be installed along the trail. Parking and restroom facilities would be provided at the trailhead.

(2) A waterbird and other wildlife viewing area adjacent to SR29. This project includes the development of a parking area, restroom facilities, interpretive exhibits, and observation decks. The wildlife viewing area would be day-use only.

(3) The development and use of a multi-agency visitor center and environmental education center adjacent to the SR29 and I-75 interchange or along the SR29 corridor.

B. The 1998 Comprehensive Conservation Plan for Florida Panther National Wildlife Refuge contains six refuge goals. Each goal has new strategies for study and management. Strategies that are new and have impacts on endangered species include:

1.1.5. Protect of 10,000 acres of adjacent panther habitat.
1.1.6. Protect approximately 360,000 acres of panther habitat with conservation easements or fee title.
1.2.8. Implement cabbage palm management.
1.2.3. Develop wildlife ponds in dryer areas.
1.3.1. Develop methods and programs to monitor panthers on a 24-hour basis.
1.4.3. Restore hydrology along I-75 canals and areas impacted on refuge.
1.4.4. Improve wading bird feeding areas near roosts.
1.4.5. Monitor eastern indigo snakes on the refuge.
1.4.6. Determine feasibility and reestablish red-cockaded woodpecker colonies.
2.3.1.1. Restore a 513-acre fallow farm field.
2.3.1.2. Restore a 40-acre fallow farm field.
2.5.1. Restore a 50-100-acre disturbed area to a moist-soil water management unit.
4.2.1. Initiate a conservation easement program for priority panther habitat.
4.2.2. Participate in multi-agency mitigation banks to protect panther habitat.
6.3. Determine the compatibility of hunting deer and hogs on the refuge.
6.4. Determine the compatibility of fishing on the refuge.

These actions are further defined in the Comprehensive Conservation Plan and Environmental Assessment.

IV.   Species and Habitats Considered:

A.   List all federally endangered, threatened, proposed, and candidate species, and describe any associated critical or proposed critical habitat that may be affected by the proposed action. Make a determination of how the proposed action may affect each.

SPECIES/CRITICAL	HABITAT	STATUS[1]	DETERMINATION[2]			RESPONSE REQUESTED[3]
			NE	NA	AA	
Florida Panther	E			X		
Wood Stork	E			X		
Bald Eagle	T			X		
American Alligator	T			X		
Peregrine Falcon	E			X		
Snail Kite	E			X		
Red-cockaded Woodpecker	E			X		
Eastern Indigo Snake	T			X		

[1]STATUS: E = endangered, T = threatened, PE = proposed endangered, PT = proposed threatened, CH = critical habitat, PCH = proposed critical habitat, C = candidate species

[2]DETERMINATION:

NE = no effect. This determination is appropriate when the proposed action will not directly, indirectly or cumulatively impact, either positively or negatively, any listed, proposed, candidate species or designated/proposed critical habitat.

NA = not likely to adversely affect. This determination is appropriate when the proposed action is not likely to adversely impact any listed, proposed, candidate species or designated/proposed critical habitat or there may be beneficial effects to these resources.

AA = likely to adversely affect. This determination is appropriate when the proposed action is likely to adversely impact any listed, proposed, candidate species or designated/proposed critical habitat.

[3]RESPONSE REQUESTED: conference, concurrence, formal consultation

V.   Determination of effects:

A.   Explanation of effects of the action: include direct, indirect, interrelated, interdependent, and cumulative effects (attach additional pages as needed):

Definitions for Effects of the Action:
Direct Effects = are those that are an immediate result of the action.

Indirect Effects = are those that are caused by the action and are later in time but are still reasonably certain to occur. They include the effects of future activities that are induced by the action and that occur after the action is completed.

Interrelated = are those that are part of a larger action and depend on the larger action for their justification.

Interdependent = are those that have no significant independent utility apart from the action that is under consideration.

Cumulative Effects = are those effects of future State or private activities, not involving Federal activities, that are reasonably certain to occur within the action area.

Florida Panther

(1)   Increased human visitation projects. The interpretive foot trail and waterbird viewing areas are located in areas that are adjacent to SR29 and are rarely used by panthers. The multi-agency visitor center is planned in a disturbed area (area was quarried for SR29 road base material) on state land at the intersection of SR29 and I-75. If this area cannot be used, another site along SR29 that is not frequented by panthers will be chosen. The visitation would be day-use only, further minimizing human/panther interactions. The projects will have beneficial, indirect effects by educating the public on the plight of the panther and alleviating the "closed to access" stigma the refuge has attained.

(2)   Other Comprehensive Conservation Plan projects. Projects 1.1.4., 1.1.5., 1.2.6., 1.2.7., 1.3.2., 1.4.3., 4.2.1., and 4.2.2. would have a direct impact on the panther as they would either protect or improve habitat that panthers use. Strategies 6.3. and 6.4. may result in increased human activities on the refuge, but the compatibility determination will consider whether these impacts are adverse to the panther.

Wood Stork, Snail Kite

(1)   Increased human visitation projects. The waterbird viewing area will directly benefit the endangered wood stork and snail kite by providing additional feeding and roosting habitat. The trail and visitor center projects will not occur in habitats used by these species. In addition, these species will indirectly benefit from the educational exhibits or information gained at the visitor center on the plight, importance, and recovery of these species.

(2)   Other Comprehensive Conservation Plan projects. Projects 1.1.4., 1.1.5., 1.2.7., 1.4.3., 1.4.4., 2.5.6., 4.2.1., and 4.2.2. would have a direct impact on the wood stork as they would either protect or improve habitat that wood storks use.

Bald Eagle

The bald eagle does not nest on the refuge. Prior to refuge establishment a nest did occur on the east side of the refuge. Occasionally, eagles are seen flying low over the refuge. It is expected that they may feed or roost on an infrequent basis.

(1)   Increased human visitation projects. The increased visitation to the peripheral areas of the refuge are not assumed to have any impact on bald eagles that may use the area.

(2)   Other Comprehensive Conservation Plan projects. Projects 1.1.4., 1.1.5., 1.4.3., 2.3.1.1., 2.3.1.2., 2.5.6., 4.2.1., and 4.2.2. would have a direct impact on the bald eagle as they would either protect or improve habitat that bald eagles use.

American Alligator, Peregrine Falcon

The alligator is found on the refuge throughout the year, while the falcon is only an occasional visitor during the fall, winter, and spring months.

(1)   Increased human visitation projects. The increased visitation to the peripheral areas of the refuge are not assumed to have any impact on alligators or falcons that may use the area.

(2)   Other Comprehensive Conservation Plan projects. Projects 1.1.4., 1.1.5., 1.2.7., 1.4.3., 2.3.1.1., 2.3.1.2., 2.5.6., 4.2.1., and 4.2.2. would have a direct impact on alligators and falcons as they would either protect or improve habitat for these species. Project 2.5.6., the moist-soil management area is expected to attract many birds and may develop into an important feeding area for wintering peregrine falcons.

Red-cockaded Woodpecker

Refuge surveys have failed to find any red-cockaded woodpeckers on the refuge, however, habitat for them does exist on the refuge. Several state and federal biologists have suggested the translocation of Naples, Florida, birds (which are being lost to development) to the refuge.

(1)   Increased human visitation projects. The increased visitation to the peripheral areas of the refuge are not assumed to have any impact on red-cockaded woodpeckers that may use the area in the future.

(2)   Other Comprehensive Conservation Plan projects. Projects 1.1.4., 1.1.5., 1.2.6., 1.4.3., 2.5.1., 4.2.1., and 4.2.2. would have a direct impact on alligators and falcons as they would either protect or improve habitat for these species. Project 2.5.1. specifically addresses the relocation of red-cockaded woodpeckers on the refuge and would greatly benefit this species.

Eastern Indigo Snake

(1) Increased human visitation projects. The increased visitation to the peripheral areas of the refuge are not assumed to have any impact on indigo snakes that may use the area.

(2) Other Comprehensive Conservation Plan projects. Projects 1.1.4., 1.1.5., 1.4.3., 1.4.5., 2.3.1.1., 2.3.1.2., 4.2.1., and 4.2.2. would have a direct impact on the eastern indigo snake as they would either protect or improve habitat for these species. Project 1.4.5. specifically addresses the study of this species on the refuge and would greatly benefit this species.

B.   **Explanation of actions to be implemented to reduce adverse effects:**
All of these species will be monitored and evaluated frequently to assure no adverse impacts occur. If adverse impacts do occur, the project and the Plan would be modified to correct that situation.

VI.

Project Leader:_____
                            Jim Krakowski   Date

VII.   **Reviewing Ecological Services Office (ESO) Evaluation:**

A. Concurrence _____   Nonconcurrence _____

B. Formal Consultation Required _____

C. Conference Required _____

D. Remarks (attach additional pages if needed):

VIII.   **Signatory Approval:**

ESO Supervisor: _____
                            Signature   Date

Note: The process ends here if the proposed action is "not likely to adversely affect".

ARD Program: _____
                            Signature   Date

ARD Ecological
Services: _____
                            Signature   Date

Note: These signatures are required for approval of a conference report or biological opinion.

References

Ashton, Jr., Ray E. and Patricia Sawyer Ashton. 1988. Handbook of Reptiles and Amphibians of Florida: Part One - The Snakes. Windward Publishing, Inc., Miami, FL. 176 pp.

Ashton, Jr., Ray E. and Patricia Sawyer Ashton. 1985. Handbook of Reptiles and Amphibians of Florida: Part Two - Lizards, Turtles & Crocodilians. Windward Publishing, Inc., Miami, FL. 191 pp.

Ashton, Jr., Ray E. and Patricia Sawyer Ashton. 1988. Handbook of Reptiles and Amphibians of Florida: Part Three - The Amphibians. Windward Publishing, Inc., Miami, FL. 191 pp.

Brandt, L. A. 1992. Wildlife sampling on the Florida Panther National Wildlife Refuge June 1990 - September 1992. Department of Wildlife and Range Science, University of Florida, Gainesville, FL. Mimeo. 30pp.

Brockman, C.F., 1986, Trees of North America. Golden Press. New York.

Burt, William H. and Richard P. Grossenheider. 1976. A Field Guide to the Mammals (Third edition). Houghton Mifflin Company, Boston, MA. 289 pp.

Clark, J., 1992, A Refuge Manager's Perspective: Refuge Management and Biological Diversity. Trans. 57th N.A. Wildl. & Nat Res. Conf.

Clinton, W.J., 1996, Executive Order: Management and General Public Use of the National Wildlife Refuge System. The White House.

Ehrlich, Paul R., D.S. Dobkin and D. Wheye, 1988, The Birders Handbook: A Field Guide to the Natural History of North American Birds. Simon and Schuster.

Felger, S. Richard. 1987. Field Guide to the Birds of North America, National Geographic Society.

Glass, Bryan P. 1975. A Key to the Skulls of North American Mammals (Second edition). Oklahoma State University, Stillwater, OK. 59 pp.

Hitchcock, A.H. 1971. Manual of Grasses of the United States. Volume One. Dover Publications, Inc., New York.

Lagler, F. Karl. 1978. Fresh Water Fishery Biology. W.M.C. Brown Company Publishers, Debuque, Iowa.

Layne, J. N. 1974. The land mammals of South Florida. Pg. 386-413 in P. J. Gleason, ed., Environments of South Florida: Present and past. Miami Geol. Soc., Memoir 2:1-452.

Metzen, W. 1985. Fakahatchee Strand: A Florida panther habitat preservation proposal. U. S. Fish and Wildlife Service Publication 64pp.

Peterson, R.T. 1961. A Field Guide to Western Birds. Houghton Mifflin Co., Boston, MA.

Porter, C.L. 1967. Taxonomy of Flowering Plants. W. H. Freeman and Company, San Francisco, CA.

Rickett, H.W. 1966. Wild Flowers of the United States. Vol. 4. Part 1. McGraw-Hill Book Company, New York.

Stebbins, RobertC. 1985. A Field Guide to Western Reptiles and Amphibians. Houghton Mifflin Co., Boston, MA.

Logan, Todd, A.C Eller, jr., R. Morrell, D. Ruffner, and J. Sewell. 1993. Florida Panther Habitat Preservation Plan - South Florida Population. Multi-agency (USFWS, FGFC, FDEP,NPS) document prepared for the Florida Panther Interagency Committee 103 pp.

U.S. Fish and Wildlife Service. 1995. Endangered and Threatened Wildlife and Plants: 50 CFR 17.11 & 17.12. U.S. Government Printing Office. 44 pp.

U.S. Environmental Protection Agency (EPA). 1985. Compilation of Air Pollutants Emission Factors, Volume 2, Mobile Sources. U.S. Environmental Protection Agency, Ann Arbor, Michigan, NTIS No. PB-205266, September.

U.S. Geological Survey. 1992. National wild and scenic river systems map. In cooperation with U.S.D.A. Forest Service, U.S. Department of the Interior, Bureau of Land Managment and Fish and Wildlife Service, and the National Park Service. December.

Whitney, S. 1985. Western Forests. The Audubon Society Nature Guides, Alfred A. Knoft, Inc., New York, NY.

Whitson, T.D., L.C. Burrill, S.A. Dewey, D. Cudney, B.E. Nelson, R.D. Lee, R. Parker. 1991. Weeds of the West. Western Society of Week Science. Pioneer of Jackson Hole, Publ.

Wood, Don. 1996. Florida's Endangered Species, Threatened Species and Species of Special Concern: Official Lists. Florida Game and Fresh Water Fish Commission. Tallahassee, FL.14 pp.

Glossary of Terms

Alternative	A refuge management pattern designed to accomplish a desired end result. May be presented in the form of refuge objectives and strategies.
Biological Diversity	The variety of life forms and processes, including the complete natural complex of species, communities, genes, and ecological functions.
Compatible Use	A wildlife-dependent recreational use, or any other use on a refuge that will not materially interfere with or detract from the purposes(s) for which the refuge was established.
Comprehensive Conservation Plan	A document that guides management decisions, and outlines management actions to be used to accomplish the mission of the System and the purposes of the refuge unit.
Conservation Easement	A legal document that provides specific land-use rights to a secondary party.
Cultural Resources	The physical remains of human activity (artifacts, ruins, burial mounds, etc.) and conceptual content or context (as a setting for legendary, historic, or prehistoric events, such as a sacred area of native peoples) of an area. It includes historical, archaeological and architectural significant resources.
Degradation	A process of transition from a higher to a lower quality of fish and wildlife habitat.
Diversity	Variety; usually used in reference to the number of species or living organisms in a given area, including some reference to their abundance.
Ecosystem	The sum of all interacting parts of plant and animal communities and their and their associated non-living environment.
Ecosystem Approach	A strategy or plan to manage the natural function, structure, and species composition of an ecosystems, recognizing that all components are interrelated, as opposed to a strategy or plan for managing individual species.
Ecosystem Management	Management of an ecosystem that includes all ecological, social, and economic components which make up the whole of the system.
Endangered Species	Any species of plant or animal defined through the Endangered Species Act as being in danger of extinction throughout all or a significant portion of its range, and published in the Federal Register.
Environment	The surroundings of a plant or animal.
Environmental Assessment	A systematic analysis of site-specific or programmatic activities used to determine whether such activities have a significant effect on the quality of the physical, biological, and human environment.
Estuary	An arm of the sea that extends inland to meet the mouth of a river.
Extinct	No longer existing.
Fauna	The animals of a particular region, taken collectively.
Flora	The plants of a particular region, taken collectively.
Fuel	Living and dead plant material that is capable of burning.
Habitat	A place where a plant or animal naturally or normally lives and grows.

Habitat Diversity	In reference to the variety in habitat; structural and compositional variety of habitat.
Habitat Management Plan	A written plan that outlines the management strategy of a plant or animal species in the area where it naturally or normally lives and grows.
Herbicide	A chemical agent used to kill plants or inhibit plant growth.
Issue	Any unsettled matter that requires a management decision.
Mitigation	Avoiding or minimizing impacts of an action by limiting the degree or magnitude of the action; rectifying the impact by repairing, rehabilitating, or restoring the affected environment; reducing or eliminating the impact by preservation and maintenance operations during the life of the action.
Mosaic	A variety of different habitats intermixed in a relatively small area. In the same manner, several successional stages intermixed within a vegetation type.
National Environmental Policy Act	An act which encourages productive and enjoyable harmony between humans and their environment, to promote efforts which will prevent or eliminate damage to the environment and biosphere, to stimulate the health and welfare of humans, to enrich our understanding of the ecological systems and natural resources important to our Nation, and to establish a council on environmental quality.
Native	This term describes plant and animal species, habitats, or communities that originated in a particular region or area, or those that have established in a particular region or area without the influence of humans.
National Wildlife Refuge System	All lands, waters, and interests therein administered by the U.S. Fish and Wildlife Service as wildlife refuges, wildlife ranges, wildlife management areas, waterfowl production areas, and other areas for the protection and conservation of fish, wildlife, and plant resources.
Prescribed Burning	The intentional application of fire to vegetation under specific environmental conditions to accomplish specific management objectives in specific areas identified in approved prescribed fire plans.
Raptor	A bird of prey such as a hawk, eagle, or owl.
Refuge Agreements	Refuge Agreements include those agreements between the refuge and other federal, state, and local entities for the operation of a multi-agency visitors' center; law enforcement; and wildfire suppression and prescribed burning.
Refuge Goals	Statements that describe a desired condition. Refuge goals are expressed in broad, general terms. They provide direction for developing objectives.
Refuge Objectives	Concise statements that describe, in measurable terms, desired conditions, and thus provide focal points for directing management activities. They describe desired conditions in greater detail than refuge goals. Refuge goals and core problems provide the basis from which objectives are developed.
Reintroduction	A plant or animal species that is introduced by humans to a range that it formerly occupied.
RONS	Refuge Operating Needs System - A refuge planning, budgeting, and communication tool.

Scoping	A process for determining the scope of issues to be addressed in the comprehensive conservation plan and for identifying the significant issues. It is a process whereby the public and federal, state, and local agencies are invited to participate.
Shrub	A plant usually with several woody stems; a bush. A shrub differs from a tree by its low height.
Species	A distinctive kind of plant or animal having distinguishable characteristics, and that can interbreed and produce young. A category of biological classification.
Stakeholder Group	A group of citizens representing a broad spectrum of interests offering business, tourism, conservation, recreation, and historical perspectives.
Strategies	Broad approaches that could be used to meet refuge goals and objectives; provide direction for defining and coordinating operational tasks to effectively perform the refuge's purpose.
Threatened Species	Those plant or animal species likely to become endangered species throughout all or a significant portion of their range within the foreseeable future. A plant or animal identified and defined in accordance with the 1973 Endangered Species Act and published in the Federal Register.
Vegetation	Plants in general, or the sum total of the plant life in an area.
Vegetation Type	A category of land based on potential or existing dominant plant species of a particular area.
Watershed	The entire land area that collects and drains water into a stream or stream system.
Wetland	Areas such as lakes, marshes, and streams that are inundated by surface or ground water for a long enough period of time each year to support, and do support under natural conditions, plants and animals that require saturated or seasonally saturated soils.
Wildlife Diversity	A measure of the number of wildlife species in an area and their relative abundance.
Wildlife Management	The art of making the land produce wildlife.

www.ingramcontent.com/pod-product-compliance
Lightning Source LLC
Chambersburg PA
CBHW081225280526
45787CB00006B/2526